Understanding
Fashion History

[

-4

-8

Understanding
Fashion History

Valerie Cumming

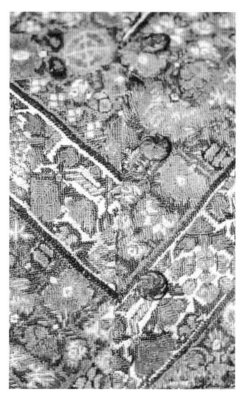

Batsford

First published 2004

© Valerie Cumming 2004

The right of Valerie Cumming to be identified as Author of this work
has been asserted by her in accordance with the Copyright, Designs
and Patents Act 1988.

Volume © B T Batsford

ISBN 0 7134 8875 1

A CIP catalogue record for this book is available from the British
Library.

Printed in Singapore
for the publishers
B T Batsford
The Chrysalis Building
Bramley Road
London W10 6SP
www.batsford.com

An imprint of **Chrysalis** Books Group

Contents

Acknowledgements and picture credits

Acknowledgements

This book has been gestating for over five years and I am grateful to everyone with whom I have discussed some of its content, though any errors in transmission are wholly mine. Several projects I have been involved with over that period have offered me opportunities to reconsider dress in different contexts, and I am grateful to Gilli Bush-Bailey, Mireille Galinou, Philippa Glanville, Ralph Hyde, Dennis Kennedy and Aileen Ribeiro for their interest as I developed these ideas. Particular thanks are due to everyone who helped me with information as I emailed and telephoned them at various stages, usually at short notice, seeking factual evidence and illustrations. My thanks go to Barbara Burman, Rosemary Harden, Anthea Jarvis, Miles Lambert, Alexandra MacCulloch, Ann Saunders, Margaret Scott, Phillip Sykas, Philip Warren and the efficient photographic library staff at the V & A Picture Library, the Museum of Costume, Bath, the National Museums Liverpool and Buckinghamshire County Museum.

I owe an especial debt of gratitude to Grace Evans and Emma Warren at Chertsey Museum for providing me with access to the Olive Matthews Collection and the other collections that they curate. Without their interest and the considerable time spent by Grace Evans on my enquiries, and the fine photography of John Chase, this book would lack crucial information and the range of illustrations that it needed. As ever, I am grateful to Batsford, in particular Tina Persaud and Roger Huggins who liked the idea for the book and never interfered in its development.

Last, but not least, I thank John Cumming, who was also writing a book but offered me unstinting support and unlimited use of the computer when it was needed.

Picture Credits

I am indebted to the following museums, collectors, publishers and institutions for the use of their images.

Bath & North East Somerset Council; Museum of Costume: Figs 26, 36, 56

Batsford Archive: Figs 3, 5, 7, 8, 15, 16, 20, 29, 51

Buckinghamshire County Museum Collections: Fig 53

Downing Collection of Textile Pattern Books at Manchester Metropolitan University: Figs 13, 54

National Museums Liverpool (Lady Lever Art Gallery): Fig 41

National Museums Liverpool (the Walker Art Gallery): Fig 59

Olive Matthews Collection, Chertsey Museum: Figs 1, 2, 9, 10, 11, 12, 14, 17, 18, 19, 21, 22, 23, 27, 28, 30, 31, 32, 33, 34, 35, 37, 38, 42, 44, 45, 46, 47, 48, 49, 50, 52, 57, 58, 60, 61, 63, 65

Private Collections Figs 4, 6, 39, 40, 55, 62, 64

Victoria & Albert Museum Picture Library: Figs 24, 25, 43

Introduction

In the late 1970s I wrote a short illustrated book for Batsford called *Exploring Costume History*. It used a traditional format in order to give students an introduction to the techniques and information they might need for undertaking projects in what was then almost always termed 'costume history'. The book gave basic instructions on how to choose and write a short project, and manageable amounts of information on male and female fashionable dress in England between 1500 and 1900. There were also sections on fabrics, technical innovations, prices, shopping and useful museum collections to visit. It was a work aimed at a specific audience – the interested reader of secondary school level and above – and it covered, if superficially, a good deal of the ground which, nearly 25 years later, I think is central to understanding the history of dress. This new book is not a revised version or even a sequel. Its aim is more ambitious in scope, using a series of thematic but linked chapters to discuss the evolution and scope of the discipline from the 1660s onwards.

In many ways that period of the late 1970s offered opportunities to all dress historians to redirect their work. A good deal of the basic knowledge was in the public domain and it was not, even then, a narrow discipline. Curators, collectors, lecturers, researchers and students had many sources of information they could use and a number of differing techniques with which they could approach the subject, but it was a relatively unfashionable area of study. The perceptions we have now about glossy designer retrospective shows, the constant media spotlight on how people look, dress and reinvent themselves with natural and surgical means were in their infancy, as was the impact of the feminist movement. The explosion of academic interest in the body, clothing and gender had not yet occurred, and practically no-one had heard of, let alone read, Roland Barthes' *The Fashion System*. There were subtle changes in emphasis, nothing seismic, and there was still a great deal to discover about what archives, collections of dress and textiles, and images in all media could tell us about the dress of the past. Of course, hindsight suggests that dress historians lacked an interlinked series of theories that would change the whole landscape of how dress *might* be studied. *Might* is an important qualification in this context because there is no agreed method for studying the subject at the beginning of the 21st century, just a great many writers, from a variety of disciplines, who are interested in carefully selected aspects of it. Such approaches can be described as a type of 'intellectual tourism', which like other forms of tourism often disregard the customs of the country that is being visited. This is not to disparage what is being attempted, but just to present a view from the perspective of those who care about all aspects of the discipline, most especially collections of dress. Curators, collectors, students and informed enthusiasts are often hard-pressed, in terms of time and opportunity, to make the case for the plurality of the subject and to argue for parity in all approaches, not just those that suggest new theories can replace all those that have gone before.

In the 1970s and 1980s there were relatively few new publications each year, unlike today when we are burdened with a mass of books dealing with the body, clothes, costume, dress, fashion and textiles. Why is this so? In part, the words themselves are central to the fragmentation of the subject. We all wear *clothes*, we *dress* ourselves, we may or may not be intrigued or amused by the vagaries of contemporary *fashion*, and given that we are not covered with fur, we cannot exist comfortably without *fabrics* or *textiles*, out of which *clothing* or *fashions* are created. This is not a word game, and it certainly is not a dictionary of terms relating to dress in all of its many forms. The main text of this book and the bibliography will point in the direction of reliable dictionaries and glossaries. Even the use of words has changed and can be confusing, being either highly theoretical or so slipshod as to suggest that any word will do, however anachronistic. Everyone wears clothes, so surely it cannot be too difficult to discuss their significance? In fact many different methods can be used, several of which have only gained acceptance in the last 25 years. Clothing can be viewed as personal property with many successive lives or as a theoretical construct, more abstract than real. The latter view fits neatly into a post-modern belief that all previous approaches lack meaning, and that historians of dress who have actually studied, analyzed and described it across several centuries have contributed little of substance to the understanding of the subject. This book will suggest that the complex history and diversity of the discipline are worthy of respect and that understanding its many strengths, as well as weaknesses, is a skill acquired incrementally by looking at, reading and thinking about evidence with an open mind.

So why and how did these changes occur over the past 25 years? How did the study of historic and contemporary dress become one of the new 'hot' subjects for academics and theorists? There are several reasons for this, one almost certainly being the fact that fashion journalism rarely adopts the critical stance found in other areas of analytical journalism, such as architecture, art, literature, music and science. This encouraged the belief that fashion has no real status as a discipline and could be absorbed into other subject areas, such as cultural history, gender studies, literary analysis and philosophy, often divorcing it from most previous texts on dress history and from surviving collections of dress and textiles. Mainstream historians, including those who study economic and social history, tended to emphasize the importance of cloth production, trade (which introduced new fabrics and techniques) and patterns of consumption. However, they rarely bothered to examine surviving dress or textiles, or even to consider their importance as evidence of changes in knowledge and skills. In his excellent *Europe, A History*, a book of over 1300 pages, Norman Davies included minimal allusions to dress in the main text, and offered three highlighted topics: the codpiece, the cravate (*sic*) and jeans.[1] The choice is amusing, but as a summary of major movements in dress history it is hardly a balanced selection.

Another reason for the fragmentation of studies related to dress and physical appearance can be traced to the blossoming of many more universities and the need to find new courses and topics to attract students. The discovery that the history of dress was relatively under-taught, and that it could be fitted into a variety of new disguises, propelled it firmly into an arena where lecturers are required to write prolifically in order to gain those much-needed research assessment points. This is not a condemnation of this development; nature abhors a vacuum, and shrewd young academics spotted this particular vacuum and began, with energy and originality, to fill it. Unfortunately it took rather too long for more traditional dress historians to spot this trend and to lobby for their approach to be taken equally seriously.

The words used to describe the study of dress history may also have contributed to the belief that it was an under-developed discipline. The Costume Society of Great Britain intermittently agonizes over whether the word *costume* is a deterrent to those who perceive clothing, dress and fashion as more inclusive words. However, the name of the society remains the same, and its distinguished history – it celebrates its 40th anniversary in 2005 – is built upon its tradition of fostering all aspects of costume, from antiquity to the present day. It has published extensively, with an annual journal, special papers and occasional conference papers. An early publication was a general bibliography in 1966, revised in 1974. This is still an excellent starting point for any student of the subject if read in conjunction with the articles, book reviews and listings that offer an annual overview of the changing approach to the discipline. In 1974, *Costume 8* offered reviews of 11 books and listed 41 recent publications. By 2003, *Costume 35* contained 25 book reviews, listed 76 new titles and in a selective list gave titles of 35 articles published in periodicals in 2002. Statistics alone do not mark shifts in approach; the change in publishing practice between 1974 and 2003 is as interesting as the quantity of reading listed. In 1974 most of the books were either produced by commercial publishers or by museums; in 2003 museums and commercial publishers were in the minority. University presses or publishers affiliated to academic institutions are now the principal publishers. In 1973 the late Janet Arnold wrote a book entitled *A Handbook of Costume* but, by 2001, the changed approach to the discipline is aptly summarized by the title of Diana Crane's book: *Fashion and Its Social Agendas, Class, Gender and Identity in Clothing*. Arnold was an admired traditional costume historian; Crane is a sociologist. Both books were well received, but other offerings by some academic authors with new theories have attracted fierce criticism for content and writing skills. Publishers cannot avoid the blame for this, as a reviewer wrote in 2001: 'Apart from more rigour in their editing, those responsible for commissioning titles and authors should remember that a good academic book is precisely the same as any other good piece of writing: its success depends on its ability to enlighten, entertain and inform.'[2] No-one would disagree with this view, but a 'good piece of writing' is not easy to achieve: it takes years of effort and practice and, of course, care in the choice of words that are used.

In 1997 in the United Kingdom there was an attempt to reconcile the differing approaches. In conjunction with the 50th anniversary of the opening of the Gallery of English Costume in Manchester, a conference was held. Its theme was 'Dress in History: Studies and Approaches', and six papers given at that conference were published in a special edition of *Fashion Theory* in December 1998 under the rather less explanatory title of 'Methodology'. Although the content of the published papers is uneven, taken together they offer a snapshot of the differing and divergent agendas of traditional and new dress historians in 1997. This is summarized succinctly in the title of John Styles' contribution: 'Dress in History: reflections on a Contested Terrain'. At this time, albeit briefly, it seemed possible that the various schools of thought might grow closer, with more co-operation between museum curators and academics, using their complementary skills, 'to recognize and embrace the conceptual diversity of current historical scholarship'.[3] A wholly admirable sentiment, but unfortunately two of the papers given at Manchester by leading costume curators did not appear in *Fashion Theory* but in *Costume*. Whatever the reasons for this, the result emphasized disunity rather than diversity. Last year I spoke to an experienced curator who was collaborating with a couple of academics on an exhibition and a book. One of the academics was the lead consultant and was to edit her work, which made her role seem reduced. I enquired whether this was a two-way street: might she be seconded to the college to teach and offer students her expertise? The answer was no. Such inequality indicates that scholarship acquired with collections is peripheral to a college curriculum, though many students undertake occasional visits to look at museum collections. The idea that academic respectability can only be conferred by a lectureship in a college, in which relevant collections are rarely if ever curated, indicates an odd set of priorities. Fortunately, changes are beginning to occur and these will be referred to later in this book.

Although there are over 100 collections in the United Kingdom, containing varying quantities of dress and textiles, the number of specialist departments is relatively few in number. Frequently such material is curated as applied or decorative arts, or as social history within much larger departments. In the 1970s and 1980s there was a general growth in museum provision in the United Kingdom, and many more displays of dress, some in designated branch museums or galleries, were opened to the public. This halcyon period was relatively short-lived and by the time of the Manchester conference in 1997, there was already a worrying downturn in the funds available for such collections. The balance was shifting against this type of collection and the expertise needed to curate it properly within museums. This left little time for hard-pressed curators 'to embrace the conceptual diversity' and use it to realign their work. Little of this was discussed in print: few dress historians have the time or the luxury of being independent enough to collate such evidence. Instead the field seemed even more open to the new approaches developing in universities in Europe and North America.

1. Brocade, French or Italian c. 1745–50
This fragment of brocaded silk has a pattern of roses on a damask ground, edged with silver lace and a lining of pink linen. Although originally acquired as a damaged stomacher, the cuts in the fabric and its curious shape are indicative of previous use on a religious effigy. It was probably acquired, as such pieces often were, as a pleasing flat textile.

2. A group of 18th- and 19th-century women's dresses
Collectors bought large quantities of dresses such as
these in the 19th and early 20th centuries. Once such
garments enter a museum they quickly become
invisible. Conservation requirements entail decisions
about the best storage conditions for individual
garments. Some can be hung on padded hangers
with supporting tapes to take weight and tissue to
prevent creasing. When they are stored like this they
are usually covered with Tyvek bags, which are inert
and do not attract dust. Other garments, textiles and
accessories have to be stored flat in trays, drawers or
boxes, interleaved with acid-free tissue and more
Tyvek or calico. The possibilities of 'open storage', or
glass-fronted storage units that enable the curators
and researchers to see their collections at a glance, is
not an option with light-sensitive and fragile textiles
of any sort. This lack of quick and easy access may
provide one of many reasons why academic writers
on dress find surviving dress incomprehensible or
disturbingly like sacred relics, cocooned in mystery.

There is no dress history equivalent to Professor Eric Fernie's *Art History and its Methods, A Critical Anthology*, which was first published in 1995 but quickly became a key text for students, reprinting four times in subsequent years.[4] This book is of relevance to anyone interested in the history of art; the glossary of concepts gives a balanced and lucid introduction to ideas that have become significant in the last 20 or so years, such as cultural history, discourse analysis and semiotics. The body of the book contains background information and short, well-chosen sections from the texts of authors writing between the mid-1550s and the 1990s. Professor Fernie's example is unlikely to be followed by a dress historian. The diffuse nature of the subject does not lend itself to a sequence of 20 or so seminal works that would provide a widely accepted academic structure and methodology. This book is not an attempt to emulate Professor Fernie's approach, and neither is it a conventional history of costume. There are already many of the latter, a number of which will be either discussed in later chapters or listed in the select bibliography.

This book is, however, an introduction to the rich and diverse literature on dress and its history, the knowledge of which has been, and can still be, relevant to anyone wishing to understand the subject. The diversity of the subject is both strength and weakness; it straddled too many disciplines from the outset, much like the Roman Empire, which even at its zenith was in decline: those who had no interest in its traditional history and methods saw its potential, while its exponents concentrated on minutiae and faced the threats to its existence ill prepared. This is a book about how dress history has been studied and an investigation of some of its many histories. Inevitably such an overview will look at extremes within the subject as well as the centre ground with which many dress historians feel most intellectually comfortable. This approach has made a standard chronology impossible. In part this is intentional: few books written in this discipline from about 1990 onwards use a chronological narrative, and the modern reader is used to thematic or modular texts.

The structure of the book allows individual chapters to be read as essays, on a range of themes that are crucial to comprehending the complexity of a subject for which there are multiple definitions. Discovering what dress is, how it has been defined, and how and why it is studied will offer traditional and some modern approaches for the reader to consider. It does, however, emphasize the links with surviving dress, which indicates the significance of material culture to the evolution and continuation of the discipline. Collections of dress and textiles offer more than attractive public displays; they are under-used resources that offer many entry points into the artistic, cultural, economic, political, social and technological trends of which they are part. Within such collections there were established hierarchies, with flat textiles being deemed more significant than textiles made into clothing during early periods of collecting. The arbitrary nature of past collecting poses problems that have to be counterbalanced with other types of evidence, but intelligent use of collections can offer insights into many aspects of the subject that theories alone cannot answer. Learning to look at surviving garments with an informed and critical attitude is an essential aspect of becoming a rounded dress historian.

The chapters on writing about dress and those on collections and how they developed precede three chapters that consider the relationship of dress to a number of areas with which it is associated. The first of these examines two interconnected areas in which the subject is frequently discussed: dress in art and dress as art. Some, if not all, art historians grudgingly accept that a thorough understanding of dress history is useful when dating works of art in which the dress and textiles are notable elements. The status of dress as an adjunct to the arts has changed with the belief in some areas that dress, or more specifically fashion, is an art. In part this reflects the closer links between all art forms in the 20th century, but the recent movement towards displaying the work of contemporary designers in major art galleries and museums has reinforced this idea.

The chapter on uniformity and disguise draws together a number of areas within which regulated or conservative styles of clothing are re-examined and reused as adjuncts to, or as inspiration for, mainstream developments in fashion. The dress, uniforms and occupational garments of the distant, intermediate or near past also provide a resource for a number of activities and enthusiasts. Clothing for re-enactment or living history, both immensely popular movements in Europe and North America, has revitalized research into the fabrics, construction and durability of historic clothing from many different periods. The actual wearing of the clothing of the recent past, not as fancy dress but as vintage elements within a personal wardrobe, contradicts any ideas that old or conservative styles deny modernity.

Costume for performance in theatres and at fairs is closely linked to the work of early historians of dress, collectors and artists, and allows consideration of how the past was represented to many different audiences. Influences between performers and their public were fluid; often the theatre was exploring and offering ideas about reform and personal presentation in advance of the views of its audiences. Throughout these essays there will be allusions to the growing interest in new theories and the impact these have had and are having upon the subject. Drawing these strands together may answer the question: what is the new dress history, and is it complementary to traditional costume history or wholly separate?

There are far too many sources of information for one book to encompass, but a range of these will be introduced within each chapter. In selecting and discussing source material of any type, the intention is to stimulate further discussion; the omission of some sources and the inclusion of others is part of this process. Surveying the entire literature of the discipline is impossible but, for the interested student of the subject and for the general reader, an overview of not just the contemporary complexity of the discipline but its long and respectable history seemed timely. Obviously much of this information can be found in reprints of classic works, both historic and modern, articles and essays in journals, in museum displays and on film but it is rarely drawn together to offer a spectrum ranging from the early work of an antiquary like Randle Holme to the schoolmarmish fashion directives of Susannah Constantine and Trinny Woodall.

The choice of dates for this book is not arbitrary. From around 1660 onwards the trading links between Europe and the rest of the known world became more dynamic, extending far beyond traditional European markets, and the importation of goods for re-export became a feature of economic life. These developments had a distinct and long-term impact on the types of fabrics, styles of dress and goods that could be acquired. In the 1660s the origins of the modern man's suit can be found, along with the establishment of an almost factory-level approach to portraiture, within which a number of conventions about timelessness and quasi-antique fashions are explored. Female performers appeared for the first time on stage in public theatres in the United Kingdom and women are found within the arts, crafts and in business. Also, and particularly significant to the central purpose of this book, from the mid- to late-17th century onwards there are more surviving examples of dress. The gradual assembling of both information and artefacts by 17th-century collectors, such as the Tradescant family and antiquaries like Randle Holme, shift the origins of the history of dress much further back than the 1830s, a date given by a recent writer on fashion history.[5]

Some explanation about the illustrations used in this book will be helpful to the reader. As it is thematic in content rather than chronological the illustrations reflect, either directly or ironically, the discussion within each chapter. All of them have been chosen because they can do at least two jobs: offer a commentary on the actual dress or fabric depicted or photographed, and indicate a context or process within which each example can be understood (methods of presentation, textile manufacture, historical allusion and so forth). There are many examples of surviving dress and textiles, and a limited number of painted, printed and photographic material in public or private collections. The emphasis on surviving dress and textiles is wholly intentional, as separately or collectively they demonstrate the relevance of such material to any study of the subject. Wherever possible the choice of black and white or colour reproduction reflects how the original illustration was made. Of course, these illustrations offer only a minute fraction of the possibilities open to the assiduous student, but they were chosen to emphasize that visual evidence and captions can offer a complementary narrative to that in the text of the book.

1680~81.

a.

Trinity Almshouses, E.

3. Drawing by Randolph Schwabe, c. 1930; pen and ink on paper
This was used as an illustration in Kelly and Schwabe's A Short History of Costume and Armour, Volume II 1485–1800. *In his text Kelly discussed the length of the coat sleeves, the cap and the shoe buckles but did not give a detailed description of the clothing. A modern dress historian might use this as an example of the unstructured nature of early men's coats and waistcoats, the excessive use of buttons, and the contrast between the formal wig, the informal ease of Captain Richard Maples's pose and the casual way in which he is wearing his clothes.*

1 Defining dress and some early authors

'Dry-as-dust fogies' and 'leisured pedants...' Kelly and Schwabe[1]

As mentioned in the introduction, words present a number of difficulties to readers interested in the clothes of the past. As a student I studied the history of dress, but when I started working in museums I worked in costume departments. Costume history was the generally accepted description of a subject that covered all aspects of display, research and writing about clothing from antiquity to the present. It had a respectable pedigree: authors in America, England, France and Germany had written standard works using the word costume in the title. Carl Kohler and Emma von Sichart's *A History of Costume* (1928, but based on Kohler's work of 1871), J R Planché's *A Cyclopaedia of Costume*, volumes 1 and 2 (1876–79), Millia Davenport's *The Book of Costume* (1948) and François Boucher's *A History of Costume in the West* (1967) indicate the usefulness of the word in English, and in translation, over a period of 100 years. However, over much the same time-span, the terms clothes or clothing, dress and fashion were used, with occasional recourse to mode (in the dictionary defined as 'a prevailing fashion or custom, practice or style'), which works less well in modern English than it does in French and German. The title of this book *Understanding Fashion History* may suggest that a word normally associated with a specific period or a development in how clothing is designed, made or distributed is being stretched to cover a past in which fashion, as a term for clothing, was not much used.

This would certainly be the view of the authors of *A Crash Course in Fashion* published in 2000. In the late 1990s the American publishers Simon & Schuster commissioned a new series of books entitled *A Crash Course* aimed at busy people who wanted, in amusing, accurate and well-illustrated short books, enough information to bluff their way in subjects such as art, design and opera. *A Crash Course in Fashion* begins with the career of Charles Worth and its timeline starts in 1850. In the discussion of Worth's contribution to fashion there is a telling, throwaway line: 'And if his designs look more like costume history than high fashion...'[2] The books on art, design and opera did not pluck an arbitrary date out of thin air, and decide that their topic must start in the 19th century or be considered tedious, but fashion history, as opposed to costume history, began with what the authors describe as 'fashion's first designer', a term wholly alien to Worth and his contemporaries. No explanation is given for discarding all previous centuries into the realm of 'costume history', but the book, like many others that appeared from about 1990 onwards, focuses its attention mainly on the post-1850 era.

The end result is pleasing to look at, but erratic as a source of information. There is a let-out clause in the introduction, which admits that, 'This book is an admittedly partisan attempt to reveal how fashion and the mood of the time fit hand in delicately embroidered kid skin glove and that to ignore the influence of what we wear is to ignore a vital element of 20th-century culture'.[3] In essence, the reader is being offered *A Crash*

Course in Modern Fashion, with centuries of achievement consigned to the dustbin of costume history without any attempt to define terms or offer guidance as to why the word fashion should be applied only to the post-1850 period. It must be assumed that neither author had heard of Samuel Pepys' description of what he called 'The king's new fashion' in 1666, or read any of the extensive modern interpretations of the use of the word in every century from the 16th to the present day.

For many readers of any book in which the word *fashion* predominates, it will conjure up the idea of supermodels and the fashion weeks around the world when contemporary designers, many of whom were trained at the influential London fashion colleges, show their new designs to the buyers and the press. In an ideal world this book would be called *Understanding Clothes* or *Understanding Dress*, but that appears to exclude fashion, all because of this problem with words. By considering the words first it may be possible to discover why some authors prefer the terms clothing, costume, dress or fashion when they write about this subject.

What is dress?

So what is the definition of dress, and why and how is it studied and written about? At the opposite end of the spectrum to the authors of the unashamedly popular *Crash Course* can be found the publicity description for a series of essays entitled *Body Dressing*. This states that: 'Dress is a crucial aspect of embodiment, shaping the self physically and psychologically ... [this book] investigates the varied ways in which western and non-western clothes operate to give the body meaning and situate it within culture'.[4] What do these words mean and are they easier to understand if a dictionary is consulted? Dictionaries are imperfect and wholly dependent upon receiving input from enthusiasts or specialists in all areas of language, but they offer a useful starting point when defining words. *The Shorter Oxford English Dictionary* tells us that embodiment means, among other things: 'the action of embodying; embodied state'; 'the concrete expression of an idea, principle etc.'; or 'the incarnation of a quality, sentiment etc'. So, when looking at embody we find: 'To put into a body'. Do we assume, therefore, that dress expresses ideas and principles or that it is put in – contained – within the body? And when clothes 'operate' is this how they produce an effect, exercise influence? And is 'situate' the same as place, position? It would be possible to continue this investigation, but the point of this exercise is to emphasize that English is a rich and remarkably flexible language and rendering it opaque rather than clear is a disservice to the reader. To translate the sentence above into everyday English might offer: 'Dress is a crucial expression of ideas and principles, which shape the individual both physically and mentally ... clothes produce effects that give the body meaning and place it within intellectual development'. But are we any closer to a useful definition? This is not a word game, but an attempt to demonstrate that the growing interest in writing about dress from authors familiar with complex linguistic and philosophical theories can be flawed by an unwillingness to write for the widest range of readers.

So, let us assume for the sake of clarity, that dictionary definitions offer a starting point. Such definitions provide a number of interlinking ideas surrounding the word dress: 'Clothing, especially the visible part of it, costume'. Clothing is described as 'wearing

4. *John the Quaker from* The Cryes of London Drawne After the Life *by Marcellus Laroon, engraved by John Savage and published by Pierce Tempest, 1688-9* Although this type of engraved material would reproduce well in black and white it did not find its way into early costume books because it was not considered an example of fashionable dress. The 74 plates in the series covered a variety of trades and occupations and provide a rare late-17th-century sequence of dated depictions of non-elite styles of London clothing for both men and women.

apparel' and costume as 'style, fashion of dress or attire (including way of wearing hair)'. Fashion is defined as 'prevailing custom, especially in dress', a route that has brought us full circle back to dress. There is no mention of embodiment, how clothes operate or where they place the clothed body in culture. These are theoretical add-ons, which are not unimportant, but they can be considered in a later chapter. Drawing together the dictionary definitions into a summary could offer this definition: dress is visible clothing, costume or wearing apparel that can imply a style or fashion, which reflects prevailing customs. This is useful because it indicates that clothing has to be visible but does not have to be fashionable. This leaves some outstanding problems: often it is necessary to know what is worn beneath clothing to interpret it correctly, so for the purposes of this book underclothing will not be excluded from the discussion, nor will accessories. The latter are defined in the dictionary as 'additional, subordinately contributive ... things', which could also be a useful definition for underclothing.

The dictionary is a useful tool when thinking about and discussing dress in all its complexities and manifestations. Today, for instance, a nightgown is something worn in bed; in the 17th century it was an informal garment, in which a person could relax in the daytime or wear among family and friends. The most useful general dictionaries for the student of dress are listed in the bibliography, but all reputable historic and modern dictionaries and specialist glossaries offer guidance to changing meanings. So, having found a plausible, if imperfect, definition of dress and its relationship within the family of terms – clothing, costume, dress and fashion – and having expanded it to include underclothes and accessories, the next step is to consider why we study it, before tackling the related question of how it is studied. The purpose of distinguishing between why and how will become clearer as this section unfolds.

Why is dress studied?

It is no coincidence, given the period covered by this book, that in England some of the most useful early sources are found in the period after 1660. The 17th century in its pre-Civil War phase can appear almost medieval in its concerns, but the last 40 years of the century contain recognizable elements of modernity in architecture, literature, public institutions, social fluidity and in philosophical and scientific thought. The first great museum collection opened to the public, and antiquarian assembling of knowledge and artefacts for both private and public use is a feature of a more analytical, enquiring intelligence. Among an array of authors who offer information about dress – diarists, letter writers, foreign visitors and playwrights – there are five of considerable significance; all are much cited and their work introduces themes that continue throughout subsequent studies of the subject and well into the 20th century.

The five authors are listed here chronologically. John Evelyn (1620–1706) kept diaries from the 1640s onwards, which were published in abridged form in 1904 and in a complete edited edition in 1955. His satirical papers on contemporary fashion were published during his lifetime. His friend, the naval administrator Samuel Pepys (1633–1703) kept detailed diaries between 1660 and 1669, which became available in abridged form in the 1820s and in their complete form in the 1970s. Randle Holme was an antiquarian whose *Academy of Armory* was published in an incomplete form in 1688. In the same year Gregory King's *Scheme of the income and expense of the several families of England* was published. Celia Fiennes (1662–1741) recorded her *Journeys*, which took place between c. 1682 and c. 1712 but were not published until 1888 (and in a more complete form in 1947). The work of these authors covers a range of professional and personal interests: individual tastes, social comment and criticism in the work of Evelyn and Pepys, with the added dimension of an intelligent woman's observation of local communities and industries in Celia Fiennes' case. The antiquarian assembling of factual information about everything from heraldry to dress in Holme's several volumes is a forerunner of many later studies. King's economic analysis of the wealth of the nation by social grouping included estimates of how much was spent on clothing and fabrics, a field that has been developed by subsequent generations of economic historians.

Pepys and Evelyn were from different social backgrounds (Pepys was the son of a tailor, Evelyn a gentleman's son), but their shared interests in science and literature drew them into a friendship that lasted until Pepys' death in 1703. Evelyn was more critical of fashion than Pepys; the latter was a natural shopper and enjoyed observing and acquiring new clothing. However, it is later generations of historians who have benefited from the publication of these diaries and of Celia Fiennes's travels. The work of Pepys and Evelyn is well known, but Celia Fiennes' *Journeys* provide a useful adjunct to the work of Gregory King, as she recorded industries throughout her travels in most English counties. She watched and described processes such as dyeing, knitting, lace making, spinning and weaving, and described the different regional products – textiles such as baize, serge, tammies, callimancoes, leather and items such as gloves and knitted stockings. She commented on quality: during her 1697 journey she wrote of Canterbury in Kent that it had '... good tradeing in the Weaving of Silks: I saw 20 Loomes in one house with severall fine flower'd silks, very good ones'.[5] However, in Honiton in Devon in 1698 she recorded that, '... they make the fine Bonelace in imitation of the Antwerp and Flanders lace, and indeed I think its as fine, it only will not wash so fine which must be a fault in the thread'.[6] Her comments on actual garments are fewer but she observes the special bathing dress worn at spas and the regional mantles of West Country women (red in winter and white in summer).[7] This observant accumulation of evidence by a wide spectrum of individuals – intrepid travellers, like Fiennes, foreign visitors, antiquarians and diarists – offers some contemporary information about dress and textiles as both an economic national strength and as indication of social customs.

Randle Holme is the first identifiable English dress historian and his work, and that of other subsequent early dress historians, is discussed in an article by Aileen Ribeiro, 'Antiquarian Attitudes – Some Early Studies in the History of Dress' published in 1994.[8] She surveyed the emergence of the subject and why it attracted a number of scholars from the late 17th century onwards. Taking Holme as a starting point and noting his considerable influence on later dress historians, she discussed the foundation of the Society of Antiquaries in 1717 as a forum within which the study of antiquities could be debated and, later, offer opportunities for publication of its members' findings (inventories and other records were a regular element in its journal). At much the same time there was a growing interest in the history of the country, not as a puny adjunct to classical studies but as a

1688.

Great
Mitton.

*5. Drawing by Randolph Schwabe, c. 1930;
pen and ink on paper*
*The caption in Kelly and Schwabe's book omitted the
details at the bottom of the drawing: 'Isabella
(Sherburne?) Gt. Mitton Yorks, Crossley pl. 6931'. This
refers to Frederick Crossley's English Church
Monuments of 1921. Kelly uses the illustration to
discuss loose kerchiefs and hoods but said nothing
else about the dress depicted. The tradition of using
drawings or re-drawings rather than photographs is
found in many early costume histories. In the late
1920s and early 1930s, if the artist was as skilful as
Schwabe, they proved a better alternative to the
more usual blurred black and white photographs.*

means of harnessing national pride. As this process accelerated in the 18th century, the customs and inhabitants of past centuries and the visual evidence that depicted them was applied to history painting. This became a source of inspiration for masquerade costumes and influenced ideas on how best to represent the historical past in the theatre. It also provided information for private collectors of costume. Once Bernard de Montfaucon's *Monuments de la Monarchie françoise* was published between 1729 and 1733 there was a natural sense of competition with the French. This included the first serious discussion of medieval French dress. An interest in medievalism, associated in the popular imagination then and now with Horace Walpole's architectural experiments and early gothic novel, was a characteristic of English antiquarian studies from the second half of the 18th century.

The first serious history of English dress, based loosely on the encyclopaedic model of Montfaucon, was written by Joseph Strutt who, using his training as an artist and engraver, made a lengthy and detailed illustrated study of all sources available to him. This resulted in his monumental works: *Compleat View of the Manners, Customs, Arms, Habits etc. of the Inhabitants of England*, published in three volumes in 1774, 1775 and 1776; and *Compleat View of the Dress and Habits of the People of England*, published in 1796 and 1799. Subsequent authors of works on monumental effigies, sculpture, arms and armour and costume acknowledged his pioneering contribution. Throughout the 19th century a number of authors offered important contributions to growing knowledge about the dress of the past and these are mentioned later in the chapter. This outline is intended only to indicate that the subject was of interest less in its own right than as a servant to other preoccupations, not least the finding, collation and publishing of new documentary and visual sources of historical evidence. The great 19th-century dress historian J R Planché – opera librettist, playwright, herald and man of letters – acknowledged his debt to Strutt and others, but also acknowledged the substantial work that others were undertaking in France and Germany. Planché's first *History of British Costume* appeared in 1834 but his masterwork appeared towards the end of his life. The two-volume *A Cyclopaedia of Costume* (1876 and 1879) appeared at much the same time as the works of a younger German dress historian, Carl Kohler.

Kohler is a useful link to the 20th century in regard to why dress is studied but, before this aspect of his work is considered, an explanation is required of the importance of French and German studies of dress. An interest in history can be antiquarian, even dilettante in its concerns, as was often the case in England, but in both France and Germany shifting political circumstances and a profound interest in issues of national identity ensured that the study of history, in all of its forms, was pursued more thoroughly and was better organized and financed. Kohler died in 1876 just five years after his book, known to us in the English edition as *A History of Costume*, was published. It was reissued in 1928 in a version edited by Emma von Sichart who, in her preface, stated that she wished '... to rescue his labours from unmerited oblivion'.[9] She provided a new introduction, excised some of Kohler's text, added new photographs and a new bibliography, in which the majority of cited publications appeared after Kohler's death; it was as much an exercise in demonstrating her scholarship as rescuing his. Kohler's book covers the period from antiquity (the Egyptians) to 1870. After considering various ancient and/or exotic civilizations, concluding with the dress of Byzantine emperors (a vast subject, neatly compressed into not quite two pages), he considers early Teutonic dress before spreading out across Europe. His interest in English dress was limited to the period between the 11th and 15th centuries but, even given this rather narrow view of the English, he must have found his information somewhere, probably in Strutt, possibly in F W Fairholt's *Costume in England*, published in 1846, or even in Charles Hamilton Smith's somewhat fancifully decorative medieval illustrations. Kohler's drawing of a late-15th-century Englishman is not dissimilar to one in Hamilton Smith's *Ancient Costumes of Great Britain and Ireland* published in two volumes in 1814.

Bibliographies, if they exist at all, offer insights into the respected scholars of a particular period. The omissions are almost more intriguing than the cited works. Sichart's bibliography lists over 40 works, the majority in German, nine in French and none in English. Omitting Planché does seem perverse, but the interesting point about this bibliography is that it is a clear reflection of how German and French scholarship led the field in dress studies for a crucial period between about 1870 and 1930. It includes Max von Boehn's *Die Mode* published in eight volumes between 1907 and 1925 and subsequently translated into English as *Modes and Manners*, about which she is effusively complimentary. However, in Sichart's words what distinguished Kohler '... is not only the detailed completeness with which [his books] cover the entire development of costume, but also the author's extensive knowledge of the practical side of the subject and his thorough familiarity with technique and cut. His work contains complete answers to all the questions that deal with the practical side of the tailor's art in bygone periods'.[10] This is hyperbole. It might, just, be possible to construct something from his diagrams and the detailed captions to the photographs of surviving examples, which are more thoroughly measured and described than in publications of a much later date. However, accurate and scaled patterns have appeared only in the last 50 years or so, and are one of the strengths of the British tradition of dress history. What Kohler pioneered was useful for theatre costumiers and, to a degree, to history painters: accuracy was related not just to depictions of past dress – in paintings, engravings and so forth – but to three-dimensional survivals.

This emphasis on the importance of accurate information for history painters and designers for the theatre will be discussed elsewhere, but a short-lived experiment of the early 1880s illustrates the significance of these two needs. Architect and theatre designer E W Godwin (1833–1886) became Secretary of 'The Costume Society, or Society for promoting the knowledge of Costume, by copying and publishing Historical Costume from Contemporary Sources only'. He was a founder member and others who joined the newly formed society in 1882 included the artists Alma-Tadema, Leighton and Whistler, the writer Oscar Wilde, the playwright W G Wills and the actors Hermann Vezin and Herbert Beerbohm Tree.[11] One of the principal purposes of the Society was to provide publications on the dress of particular periods, but after producing one on medieval dress in 1883 it seems to have collapsed.[12]

The growing emphasis on study for the purposes of making accurate costumes for the theatre, to assist history painters and for fancy dress propelled the subject into a cul-de-sac of what, unfairly or otherwise, was considered a minor craft skill. Talbot Hughes's collection

A Lady of Quality in her somer dress.

6. A Lady of Quality in her Somer dress; *black and white engraving by unknown artist c. 1686*
The plate is inscribed 'Sold at the White Horse without Newgate' and is from the cover of Mary Watton's chapbook. This engraving is a pirated version of one of the licensed French fashion illustrations, and is used as an eye-catching cover for the modest books sold by hawkers. The carefully depicted style of dress and hood present additional information about female clothing in the late 1680s that is not visible in Schwabe's drawing of the 1688 funerary effigy.

of historical costume and accessories was presented to the Victoria & Albert Museum after being exhibited at Harrods in 1913.[13] He had spent a good deal of time undertaking research as well as collecting, and produced a strange book: *Dress Design, An Account of Costume for Artists and Dressmakers*. This was issued in The Artistic Crafts Series of Technical Handbooks and was wholly practical in intention; my copy has the stamp of Borough Polytechnic Girl's Trade School. Though he had obviously seen Kohler's book, as his approach to layout, illustrations, line drawings and diagrams was similar, he gave no bibliography, so this cannot be known for sure. The inaccurate pastiche re-drawing of original paintings, prints and sculptures popularized a form of illustration that has been, intermittently, a feature of the subject ever since and is much inferior to earlier examples. It is easy to criticize with hindsight and no-one today would be bold enough to attempt a book that covered prehistory to c. 1860 in 364 pages packed with a mass of different types of illustration. Despite his years of study he seems to have lacked a discerning eye. Separated by just a few pages are two photographs: one is captioned, 'Portrait of a Lady in Embroidered Costume. Between 1620 and 1640'; the other, 'Linen Male Jacket Embroidered with Gold and Silk. 1600–40'. What he had separated, unwittingly, was the portrait of Margaret Laton of 1620 and the embroidered jacket she wore when painted.

This sidelining of historic dress from the mainstream academic respectability it had enjoyed in the 18th and 19th centuries irritated authors of the next generation. When Francis M Kelly and Randolph Schwabe's *Historic Costume, A Chronicle of Fashion in Western Europe, 1490–1790* was published by Batsford in 1925, the review in *The Queen* described it as 'Intended primarily for the costumier, film producer, and artist, it is full of delight for the ordinary reader, who will find it an excellent help in the pleasant game of trying to construct a livelier vision of the past'.[14] When the two authors went on to produce *A Short History of Costume and Armour* in two volumes in 1931, the prefaces in both volumes indicated their frustration with their contemporaries' understanding of why the dress of the past was being studied. The preface to volume I (1066–1485) states, 'The study of costume has heretofore been associated with dry-as-dust fogies on the one hand, on the other with "period" plays, historical genre-painting, and the like'.[15] However, in the introduction they mention that designers for stage and film, illustrators and painters need an understanding of tailoring, cut and drapery and refer them to the bibliography and 'the several modern costume-books which have devoted considerable attention to such questions'.[16] This advice is cross-referenced in the bibliography, indicating which works they recommend: Herbert Norris in English; Adrien Harmand, Albert Racinet and E Viollet-le-Duc in French; and Kohler and Carl Masner in German. Although their two volumes deal principally with dress in England their bibliography has practically no works in English by their contemporaries; only the second volume of Herbert Norris's *Costume and Fashion, From Senlac to Bosworth* (1927) merits a mention. The other English works they list are much earlier: F W Fairholt's *Costume in England* (originally published in 1846 but the 1896 edition is recommended); D C Calthrop's *English Costume* published in four volumes in 1906; H W Lonsdale and E J Tarver's *Illustrations of Medieval Costume* 1874; Planché's *British Costume* and his two-volume *Cyclopaedia*; and Strutt's *Dress and Habits* in the edition by Planché, published in 1842.

Perhaps even these classics of the past were inadequate, for Kelly and Schwabe launched into another tirade in their preface to volume II (1485–1800). This was longer than the first and is worth quoting in full:

'Except as a pastime for leisured pedants, the study (?) of costume has hitherto subserved no more serious end than that of an excuse for fancy dress, or an embellishment of "historic" pageants, stage and film productions, book-illustration etc. It is gradually being realized that, logically pursued, it forms one of the most valuable criteria we have in dating examples of the art of the past; and even determining their attribution. Many a hoary impostor, long enthroned in general esteem by a succession of "popular" picture-books, would long ago have been relegated to its proper place, had it been confronted with this test'[17].

There is palpable anger in these words but it is difficult to know whether it was provoked by intellectual unease at the obvious superiority of French and German scholarship or by

7. Drawing by Randolph Schwabe; pen and ink on Japanese vellum, c. 1927
There are few illustrations of surviving dress in Kelly and Schwabe's books. An exception is this white satin wedding dress of 1760, on display at the Victoria & Albert Museum, London, in 1927. The caption described it as 'The "Watteau pleat"' with the brisk words in the text adding, 'the so-called "Watteau pleat" (wholly foreign, by the way, to Watteau's art and age)'. The accuracy of these drawings was admired by Millia Davenport, who cited Kelly and Schwabe's books as the exceptions to her aversion to line drawings in books on costume. The difficulty is that unless the illustration is thoroughly captioned there is no way of knowing practical details such as fabric and colour.

8. Illustration from Edward Baines, History of the Cotton Manufacturers in Great Britain, 1835.
The Quennells used this type of illustration in their books for children to offer context to their discussion of clothing. They used a Baines illustration of power loom weaving and another of yarn preparation in 1791 opposite the page on which 19th-century clothing was discussed. Block- and roller-printed calicos were used for clothing and soft furnishings.

the type of lightly disparaging remarks with which many dress historians are familiar, as if studying 'old clothes' were less significant an element in understanding history than 'old' paintings, engravings, ceramics, furniture and metalwork. Being linked with the practical requirements of stage and film designers rather than being perceived as serious contributors to art historical research was obviously irksome. They looked at many different sources of visual information, including collections of arms and armour, but there are few examples of surviving dress among their illustrations, and a postscript to their last volume compressed advice on examining textiles and costume into one sentence.[18]

While Kelly and Schwabe were arguing for the subject to be taken more seriously, but not much considering surviving dress as a factor in why dress is studied, other non-specialist authors had a broader-based approach. Marjorie and C H B Quennell were prolific popularizers of history in the 1920s and 1930s. Their books, written in three- or four-volume sets, were aimed at children but reviews of the time suggest that adults found them equally appealing. Taking just one example of their work, the third volume in *A History of Everyday Things in England*, 'The Rise of Industrialism 1733–1851', indicates the inclusive nature of their approach. Part I discussed farming, building, clothing, subsidiary trades and sanitation in the period 1733 to 1800, and part II followed the same pattern. What is interesting is that clothing is discussed and illustrated within the context of technological change. Clothing is placed alongside explanations of spinning, weaving, the invention of Kay's shuttle and the work of Hargreaves, Arkwright and Crompton. The reader is given a list of recommended museums, all three of which are in London: the Victoria & Albert Museum and its out-station Bethnal Green Museum, and the London Museum. This placed the understanding of dress squarely within an economic, social and technical history, and illustrations of dress are preceded or interspersed with clear drawings of how shuttles, the Spinning Jenny and other machines worked. The dress history might be cursory and the re-drawn illustrations somewhat whimsical, but this joined-up approach with its acceptance that museum collections were of importance alongside social and technical change, was well in advance of its time.

Kelly and Schwabe were pioneers because they wanted the subject to be taken seriously in the context of the fine arts. Kelly's organization of information was still being copied, albeit refined, decades later by the Cunningtons and others, and Schwabe's excellent drawings (he was Principal of the Slade School of Fine Art) set a standard that many tried to emulate. However, despite their considerable legacy this was yet another cul-de-sac. Their approach to the history of dress concentrated on a narrative of 'high fashion' and was descriptive in regard to what a painting, an engraving or a sculpture might yield in terms of information about date and content. The more rounded approach written for children by the Quennells offered many more opportunities for placing dress within processes of change and evolution. As an interest in surviving garments developed among collectors and in museums, the reasoning behind the study of the subject began to change. This led to a transitional phase in which *why* it was studied and *how* it was studied were seen as no longer a straightforward accumulation of materials and sources principally found among documents and in the fine arts.

The historians of dress who saw their role as informed interpreters of dress in paintings had a skilful advocate in the next generation. James Laver worked at the Victoria & Albert Museum in London in the department of prints, drawings and paintings, of which he eventually became Keeper. He used the resources of that institution and contacts in other museums and galleries to commence a career, from the mid-1920s onwards, of writing extensively about dress from the perspective of someone who was interested in the reasons for changes in fashion; he was an amalgam of art historian and theorist, in effect a new type of dress historian, whose work in the latter sphere will be discussed in the next chapter.

In 1947 he organized an exhibition for the National Book League called The Literature of Fashion, which ran from 21 November 1947 to 3 January 1948. Laver's exhibition was accompanied by a short booklet, which offers an insight into his views at that time. The introduction quickly differentiated between the Literature of Fashion and a bibliography of costume. His definition was succinct: 'The history of Costume is as old, or almost as old, as the history of Humanity – and this whether we take the anthropological or the Biblical view. Fashion is a matter of the last few hundred years, but to understand why this should be so will take us into some very deep waters.'[19] The 'deep waters' are concerned with Laver's theoretical ideas, and in particular his term 'the Seduction Principle', which is discussed in the next chapter. The booklet placed each item within distinctive sections, each section being given a short, explanatory preface, and a comment about the merits of each book in his bibliography. The sections within which the books are listed are fairly

9. Day dress, English c. 1809–12
The dress is cotton with a design of sprigs, the neck, cuffs and hem edged with woven geometrically patterned braid in similar colours to the sprigs. In his classic book English Women's Clothing in the Nineteenth Century, published in 1937, C W Cunnington used a small number of coloured photographs of garments from his collection with one-line descriptions. The date of this dress would place it in the period 1808 to 1821, which Cunnington described in the section on Fashions and Sex Attraction as 'Debased classic' and of 'Modified exhibitionism'. His sub-Freudian ideas on why women wear clothing are patronizing, but the book's factual content is still of great use.

10. Day dress, English c. 1809–12 (detail)
This detail highlights the design on the printed cotton, the braid edging and the back fastening. The apparent simplicity of this early-19th-century style did not extend to unaided fastening. In Cunnington's books such details would have been drawn rather than photographed.

comprehensive: General Works published before 1800; General Works published after 1800; a series of Works on Special Periods – Medieval, 16th Century, 17th Century, 18th Century, 19th and 20th Centuries. Subsequent sections offer: Philosophy, Psychology and Criticism; The Art of Dress; Technical; Children's Costume; Corsets; Hats and Hairdressing; Riding Habits; Fans; Learned Periodicals; Bibliographies and Catalogues; Periodicals; and Pictures, Drawings and Prints.

Inevitably there are titles in French and German, but many more in English than might have seemed feasible to Kelly and Schwabe less than 20 years earlier, including works by American authors, and books on social and art history of use to the dress historian. It is interesting to compare Laver's notes on each title to those given by Pegaret Anthony and Janet Arnold in *Costume, A General Bibliography*, published nearly 20 years later. Some reassessments had taken place but the essentials had not much changed apart from the addition of more recent works, including many by Laver. In 1947 his categories suggest why and how he thought 'fashion' might be studied. The narrative historical sections occupy about half of his booklet with the areas of special interest, from philosophy to fans, segmented rather arbitrarily. He has no section on accessories, just hats and fans, thus omitting a range of possibilities – gloves, jewellery, shoes – all of which had been published in book form by that date. However, as an overview it is useful. It indicates a substantial body of information, uneven in content and scope, but with a healthy tradition drawn from American, British and European research. It also presents a relatively small world of like-minded individuals, all of whom, in their different ways, were adding to the discipline within its various narratives. Laver knew everyone of note involved with dress history – Andre Blum, Norah Bradfield, Iris Brooke, the Cunningtons, John Nevinson, and many more. The subject was no longer the domain of men and Laver acknowledged the contribution of women who were not just his contemporaries but who came from earlier generations, though with the occasional caveat about their lightweight scholarship or dubious drawing skills.

Although Laver paid fulsome tribute to C W Cunnington in his notes on authors, he makes no reference to the fact that in 1947 the Cunnington collection found a home and a place of public display in Manchester, England. Costume in museums was, as yet, an underdeveloped resource for study and publication. In the very short section of his booklet devoted to bibliographies and catalogues there are seven entries and only one is a real attempt at a catalogue: *London Museum Catalogue No. 5 Costume*, originally published in 1933, and reissued in 1935 and 1946. Laver described it as 'fully annotated catalogue of this important collection of *dresses*...' [my italics], but makes no further comment about the future potential of museum catalogues or their place within the literature of the subject.[20] The transition from *why* we study costume to *how* we study it had gained new possibilities in the form of collections of garments, and not just dresses, held in the public domain. However, at more or less the same time that James Laver was listing books, many of which were illustrated with line drawings of varying degrees of skill and accuracy, the great American scholar of dress, Millia Davenport, was completing her massive *The Book of Costume*, published in two volumes in 1948. It is an informative and wide-ranging narrative on the history of dress from prehistory up to 1860. Her first introductory remarks defined a new approach and it is worth quoting them in some detail:

'Years of work, research and study in the field of costume have led me to three conclusions about books on costume which I do not think are valid for me alone.
1. Books illustrated by the author are usually to be deplored, and many of them are terrible.
2. The best book is the one with the most pictures, all of them contemporary documents; the best text is based on the words of contemporaries – friends, enemies, or travellers.
3. The physical location or source of every picture, and the number of every manuscript should be given, if possible, as a help in finding colored reproductions, further information, or more illustrations from a series.
The ideal book of costume, to my way of thinking, would provide so many pictures (all documents, arranged chronologically, and in color) that the story would tell itself without words.'[21]

It was and is a monumental work of scholarship and although knowledge has advanced and opinions have changed since 1948, its reissue as a one-volume work in 1972 created a new and equally receptive audience. Occasionally its origins (it was intended to be a dictionary before the author changed her mind) can be seen in groups of watches, fans, fashion plates and similar, which are interspersed between photographs of paintings, prints, drawings, manuscripts, sculptures, ceramics and other original sources of illustration. It is genuinely encyclopaedic and although there have been attempts to overtake it, it is unlikely to be replaced; the sheer expense of paying for illustrations would render such an exercise prohibitive. Alas, despite Millia Davenport's desire to use only original sources of illustration, some photographic prints were not of the best quality and it is sometimes impossible to see the details to which she refers in the accompanying text. Despite this she was blazing a trail that set a new standard for major works on dress history written by women rather than men.

In 1948 it probably did not occur to Millia Davenport that she was, intentionally or otherwise, demonstrating that female scholars were equal to if not better than the assorted men who had previously written major works on dress. She was aware of the achievements of women and what they had contributed to the discipline before her, but it seems unlikely that she saw a line between the genders; it was the quality of the work that mattered. Historically, however, she sits squarely on the cusp that defined dress studies: gradually the discipline was being ceded to women in many aspects of its study.

How is dress studied?

In the previous section, there seemed inevitably to be an overlapping of *why* dress was studied with *how* it is studied. Antiquarians, academics and enthusiasts were keen to find evidence that might assist those who needed clear and accurate illustrative information about how the dress of the past looked and the social context within which it evolved. Today, if we decided to investigate how the fashions of previous generations were recorded, we might just bury ourselves in a good library, surf the net or, if we are equipped to do so, devise questionnaires, arrange discussion groups, study newspapers, magazines, films and television – anything which might assist our comprehension of both past and present. All of these methods cannot recapture the past without imposing upon it our system of values. We look at a multiplicity of sources, such as archives, books, images, material culture, and from them create constructs that suit modern sensibilities: ethnicity, gender studies, inclusiveness and other contemporary issues. Our predecessors were not less sophisticated but they were more fortunate; they found information afresh. They delved into unsorted archives, drew tomb effigies, copied sculptures, studied manuscripts, gazed at portraits and, occasionally, found clothing or textiles that seemed to belong within their period of interest. The evidence was either outside the public domain or unsorted. It was pure, unadulterated detective work – sifting, collating and following up leads from fellow scholars. This, in part, explains the uncontextualized publications that marked the early endeavours of historians of dress; they were caught up in the excitement of collation rather than explanation and context.

Slowly, from the late 19th century – Kohler's work is important here, yet again –primitive methodologies were acquired in the study of dress. These tend to relate to the perceived application of material found and presented in public, or at least within scholarly circles. No source material was omitted as every category of artefact from the fine and decorative arts had the potential for adding to visual knowledge; published and archival literary sources were scoured for useful information; comparative records were kept, assisted by the introduction of photography in the sphere of visual material. Garments began to be described, measured and inspected for technical innovation. The emphasis, however, was on the development of fashion; little attention was paid to the clothing worn outside elite social groups, although armour, ecclesiastical vestments, livery and uniforms were included.

The notion of progress and perfectibility, ideas that appealed to the Victorians, could be applied to changes in how elite dress was studied over the course of many centuries. However, describing the past objectively did not necessarily prepare these early dress historians for absorbing critical new approaches to the fashions of their contemporaries. Dress reform movements, from about 1850 onwards, attracted both determined advocacy and popular derision. This focus on innovations such as Bloomers, Jaeger underclothes and aesthetic dress offered the heady idea that fashionable dress was controversial and worthy of study, if only to place it within a longer historical narrative. It was usually female dress that attracted criticism for both aesthetic and practical reasons. The quasi-scientific fascination with the supposedly unnatural constraints of corsetry and the potential health hazards posed by pursuit of the perfect silhouette were elements in a growing emphasis on the history of women's dress. Although in the 1920s it was male dress reform that was under discussion, the collectors and writers of the post-1918 period rarely paid the same amount of attention to men's clothing as they did to women's when assembling data on clothing of the recent past. Even when dress, both contemporary and historic, was subjected to economic and psychological theories, as in the work of Flügel, Freud and Veblen, discussed in chapter 2, masculine appearance was perceived to be much less worthy of study and analysis.

The most obvious changes in the study of dress after 1900 occurred because many more museum collections were being assembled, studied and displayed. The contents of these collections presented opportunities to compare and contrast – the process by which it was discovered if surviving garments bore any relationship to how they were depicted in

11. Day dress, English c. 1855–60
The fabric of this dress is muslin with overchecks of
opaque lines, and printed with roses and leaves.
Millia Davenport used photographs of surviving dress
in The Book of Costume, including some in displays
at the Metropolitan Museum of Art, but none were
colour illustrations.

drawings, paintings, prints and fashion plates. These collections allowed investigation of the impact of technical changes in dyes, machinery and fabrics, and consideration of the contribution of factory production and how an increase in ready-to-wear garments in a new style of shop affected the buying of clothes. The opportunities seemed almost limitless and criticisms that the collections being assembled were untypical, eclectic and really only useful for chronological displays of the evolution of fashionable styles across two to three centuries were ignored; the same criticisms might be levelled at almost every other sort of collection.

A major problem was the lack of an accepted method of training for dress historians, even when the materials for study enlarged and their use became more diverse. The discipline did not find its way into higher education easily. Students of art history and history might discover the subject by chance, but were rarely offered lectures or the option to study it systematically. In art colleges, especially those with theatre design departments or training for students who wanted to enter the fashion trades, it played a small part and it crept onto the syllabuses of teacher training colleges, often allied to the study of needlework and dressmaking. Many skilful early curators and lecturers acquired knowledge by devising their own study methods because there was no agreed curriculum and no methodology. Many costume curators came from backgrounds in history, art history and archaeology, but if they had no senior colleague/s to advise them, they also found that the literature was thin. They probably had to acquire whatever books they could afford, but catalogues of collections were almost non-existent. Finding out about what was in collections often involved visiting them and examining items. Very few exercises in listing and comparing the contents of dress and textiles collections have ever taken place and probably the most thorough attempt to discover the contents of British collections was Janet Arnold's, published in *The Handbook of Costume* in 1973. In that she admitted that the coverage was not complete and more than 30 years later the collections she described have grown in size and increased in number.[22]

One measurement of the success of a discipline, apart from general histories, catalogues and public displays, is if it can provide enough content and debate to maintain a specialist journal. University and subscription libraries have shelves groaning with this type of publication. History in all of its many manifestations – artistic, economic, political, social and cross-disciplinary studies – provides the content for endless new interpretations. Such journals are a record of changing interests in how a subject is studied, but it was not until 1967 that a regular English-language journal, *Costume*, the annual journal of The Costume Society, was first published in the UK. The 1967 edition is short but offers something of a 'mission statement' to use a modern phrase: '...to promote the study and preservation of significant examples of historic and contemporary costume. This embraces the documentation of surviving examples, the study of decorative arts allied to the history of dress, as well as literary and pictorial sources'.[23] This was a broadly based indication of all the available methods used at that time. The editorial included a request for articles 'or suggestions for articles, from all those interested in the enthralling subject of Costume, whether or not they are members of the Society'[24]. The Secretary's Letter adds that, 'All costume specialists grumble that publishers want the same old hack "costume through the ages" and will not publish their work on the particular topic which preoccupies them. Here is your captive audience, your own publication – take advantage of it'[25] The four short articles indicate some of the range of information that the journal hoped to publish. Colin Ford, at that time Deputy Curator of the National Film Archive in the UK, introduced readers to the archive as a source of information from 1895 onwards, with its opportunities to see people '...wearing clothes, walking and running in clothes, relaxing and working in clothes'.[26] Although he admitted that he was not an expert on costume he made the shrewd point that '...costume is not a static thing and it is impossible to understand fully its developments and changes without seeing what people did in that costume and what therefore induced them to alter it'.[27] While opening up new possibilities for how 20th-century dress could be studied, he said that there was a lack of funding, a shortage of viewing machines, a need to restrict access to 'serious researchers and bona fide students' and a charge of two guineas an hour for the privilege. This effectively closed down this option to all but the comparatively wealthy at a time when videos and DVDs were unimagined.

The other three articles covered more traditional sources of evidence. Daphne Bullard, then Keeper of Worcestershire County Museum, wrote about the strengths and mentioned some of the weaknesses of the costume collection housed at that time in Hartlebury Castle. There is a brief history of how the collection was assembled; like a number of others it benefited from the collecting zeal of a particular individual. The article is illustrated by two of her own drawings, both full page, one of a woman's muslin dress of 1815, the other of a man's linen frock(coat) of 1810. The next contribution, written by John Dony, provided a selective bibliography on straw hats. The final piece, by Janet Arnold, combined a drawing, description and detailed pattern for the wedding dress worn by Princess Sophia Magdalena of Denmark when she was married in Sweden in 1766. These accurate and scaled patterns, a feature of Janet Arnold's work throughout her career, set a new standard in how a practical dress historian could provide exactly the type of information needed by theatre, film and television designers. At that stage in her writing career she was less interested in placing the dress within its cultural and social history, so the modern reader has to consult a Swedish history to discover the identity of the groom.[28]

These early contributions, with their four examples of how dress could be studied – using museum collections, printed and archival information and film – are still relevant today. However, in nearly 40 years the journal has widened its scope to cover dress, textiles and accessories of every period, many countries and continents, dress of all social classes and occupations, uniform, theatre costume and the work of fashion designers past and present. It has reviewed books and exhibitions and provided selections of articles published in other journals both in English and other languages. As a commentary on how dress has been studied since the late 1960s it is an important English-language resource alongside *Dress* (the journal of the Costume Society of America), *Textile History* and a wide variety of journals and newsletters published by societies that specialize in aspects of dress, design and textiles within more tightly defined periods.

2   Theories and the new dress history

'A scientific treatise on the evolution of fashion is indeed long overdue. It is not extravagant to ask that this almost universal human phenomenon, clothes, may some day receive a little of the reasoned, analytical and constructive study which has in the past been lavished upon earthworms, pigeons and even potsherds'. Dr Mortimer Wheeler[1]

Few writers have ever seriously suggested that fashion is a science, but since the early 1980s it has certainly become of increasing interest to social scientists and commentators from disciplines influenced by the social sciences. This chapter will use a combination of recent and less recent examples to allow consideration of the varying approaches that have evolved over the last three decades. Theories about dress are not, however, the recent phenomenon that some modern fashion writers might lead us to believe. From the early 19th century onwards the subject attracted theoreticians from diverse backgrounds and although their ideas have since been challenged, they form part of the evolution of the subject.

When Dr Mortimer Wheeler wrote the words at the beginning of this chapter in 1933, he was familiar with at least one theorist of dress history, as they would be known today. He cited Thomas Carlyle's Professor Diogenes Teufelsdröckh as '...the one and only philosopher of clothes'.[2] Carlyle's *Sartor Resartus* had appeared in essay form exactly 100 years earlier, and although there had been other theorists since then, there is no reason why Wheeler should have read them since he was a distinguished archaeologist and more familiar with

12. Detail of a woman's waistcoat c. 1730
The fabric is silk satin quilted with silk threads and embroidered with flower motifs, padded interlining and printed calico lining. Work on the waistcoat preparatory to a display has revealed that the garment has been relined. The original lining complements the silk embroidery and edging, whereas the second lining has discoloured and faded. This type of careful investigation during or prior to conservation and display is consistent with a modern interest in discovering the previous 'lives' of a garment. In this instance the later lining has not been removed as there is a good visual and documentary record of the garment for research and publication purposes.

potsherds. In a recent book, *Fashion Classics, From Carlyle to Barthes*, the Australian academic Michael Carter explored the contribution made by eight theorists. Carlyle (1795–1881) was a historian and essayist; Herbert Spencer (1820–1903) a social philosopher; Thorstein Veblen (1857–1929) an economist; Georg Simmel (1858–1918) a sociologist and social philosopher; Alfred Kroeber (1876–1960) an anthropologist; John Flügel (1874–1955) a psychoanalyst; James Laver (1899–1975) spent his professional career curating prints and drawings in the Victoria & Albert Museum in London; and Roland Barthes (1915–80) is usually described as a cultural critic and literary theorist. Four of these figures worked in England (Carlyle, Spencer, Flügel and Laver); Veblen and Kroeber were Americans; Simmel was German and Barthes French. Their origins and disciplines brought a blend of British, European and American intellectual analysis to a subject that, as we saw in chapter 1, was still closely linked to the needs of art historians, early costume curators, theatre designers and costumiers. The early- to mid-20th century shift in emphasis to collecting and to museums within which costume was displayed had, superficially, little to do with theories evolved by anthropologists, economists and sociologists. So, although costume curators did not exactly neglect this area, theoretical ideas on dress/fashion were re-examined and had more impact within academic research in universities.

Laver's legacy

In the early to mid-20th century, there was no obvious route for anyone wanting to study the dress of the past. Many people came to the subject by accident, perhaps because their job required expertise that had to be acquired piecemeal, or out of enthusiasm such as that shown by great collectors like C W Cunnington and Doris Langley Moore. Early theoreticians came from disciplines not usually associated with mainstream dress history and had an uneven impact on more traditional writers. In Laver's booklet of 1947, in the section on psychology, he only lists Flügel and himself, seeming not to know of or value the contribution made by those already published whom Michael Clark discusses with exemplary clarity in *Fashion Classics*. Over 20 years later, the revised edition of *Costume, A General Bibliography* (1974) similarly only lists Flügel, even more books by Laver and far too many by C W Cunnington. Dr Cunnington, resourceful and knowledgeable though he was, had little theoretical interest in anything beyond an enquiring curiosity about *Why Women Wear Clothes*, the title of one of his many books.[3] The work that needed to be done to ensure that costume was seriously studied and displayed within a museum context, which was of importance to Cunnington, his contemporaries and the generation after them, meant that they accepted rather than challenged the few theoretical studies available to them.

Up until the 1970s traditional teaching about the history of dress, whether formal or informal, might have included some consideration of economic and psychological theories. The two most influential texts were Thorstein Veblen's *The Theory of the Leisure Class* (1899) and J C Flügel's *The Psychology of Clothes* (1930). Veblen's ideas can be summed up pithily as a theory of 'conspicuous consumption'. He perceived the women's fashions of the 1890s as conspicuous manifestations of expense and waste, indicative of the tastes of idle and mindless women with rich husbands. In the words of a modern writer on fashion, Veblen offered: '...explanations of capitalism that equate men with production and women with consumption'.[4] Flügel, building upon work done by Havelock Ellis in the late 19th century, was not particularly interested in fashion but in the sexual signals given by the clothed female body and the idea of 'shifting erogenous zones', as changing fashions emphasized or revealed particular parts of the female anatomy. He devised another theory about men's clothing called the Great Masculine Renunciation. This flawed idea suggested that men adopted sober business-like suits from the mid-19th century as an indication of their 'immunity from frivolous distraction', in other words the constantly changing styles and colours of female clothing.[5]

Veblen and Flügel's ideas interlock so neatly, offering economic and psychosexual patriarchal views of women's frivolity and subjugation, which it is hardly surprising, proved popular with male dress historians such as C W Cunnington and James Laver. Laver developed his ideas on the Hierarchical Principle (dressing to indicate one's position in society), the Utility Principle (dressing for warmth and comfort) and the Seduction Principle (dressing to attract the opposite sex) as a result of Flügel's work. The first two categories related primarily to men's attitudes to clothing and the last to women's. In 1947 he was musing somewhat sadly that if women pursued 'their career of "emancipation" until they have all landed themselves at the factory bench ... it is unlikely that they will ever bedeck themselves in the frills and furbelows of former ages'.[6] However he rallied to decide that, 'The Seduction Principle still rules in women's dress. Their clothes are still alive, representing as they do the principle of Life itself'.[7] This view might be excused as the idealization of a lost world of decorative and unchallenging femininity in the grey post-War years of rationing, but over 20 years later, in the final paragraph of his classic *A Concise History of Costume* (1969), which takes the story up to 1968, he wrote that the Seduction Principle might outlive the Hierarchical Principle and the Utility Principle in the clothing of both sexes.[8] Laver's book was reprinted in 1982 and reappeared in 1995 under a new title: *Costume and Fashion, A Concise History*. The book's last chapter was rewritten to bring it up to date, and in 2003 it was further revised. The Seduction Principle was omitted and a brisk narrative covering the developments of the period from 1940 replaced all theory, however dated or modern. There was no explanation about either the title change or the omission of Laver's pet theories. Today, undoubtedly, it takes inordinate bravado and self-confidence for a man to support the Seduction Principle. Though, in the world of fashion, at least one major designer is perfectly comfortable with it. In an interview in 2003, John Galliano explained that, 'My goal is really very simple. When a man looks at a woman wearing one of my dresses, I would like him basically to be saying to himself, "I have to fuck her" ... I just think every woman deserves to be desired'.[9] Feminist hackles might rise at such uncompromising honesty, but undoubtedly modern fashion design, despite all the theoretical spin put on it by academics, is often provocatively sensual.

An 'internalized' approach?

Historians, in particular those who write about art, economic or social history, have often included some discussion of dress or textiles, though not with any great accuracy, seeming to believe that most books and collections are of dubious research merit. The economic historian Negley Harte wrote in 1976 that, '...the history of fashion has been conceived either in an exclusively "internalised" way, or has derived its flavouring of economic and social significance only from the easy pickings of literary quotation or from an added dash of amateur psychology'.[10] This may have been intentionally provocative, a call for a fresh approach, but such criticism was hardly justified then but even less so now, as the opportunities to study and write about the history of dress and textiles, or areas allied to them, have multiplied since the mid-1970s. Before considering the acceleration of interest and new work since the 1970s it is worth trying to find out what this 'internalized' method of study might be.

Anyone exploring the shelves of museums, art galleries and some large bookshops will find whole sections devoted to 'fashion', a word now more acceptable than costume at least to booksellers. Alongside the glossy books on leading fashion designers, the basic introductions for children with their re-drawn or fanciful illustrations of the dress of the past, there are considerable numbers of reprints of classic authors from the 19th and early 20th centuries: Kelly and Schwabe, Norris, Planché, Racinet and others are available to the interested reader. These reprints sit alongside more recent classics, which are hardly ever out of print: the works of Nora Waugh and Janet Arnold which did so much from the 1950s onwards to make accurate patterns and details of construction available to theatrical costumiers, interpreters at historic sites, re-enactors and to museums who offer visitors the fleeting experience of wearing an approximation of the dress of the past rather than just looking at it. If this is 'internalized' it has been enormously successful at assisting the public understand rather more about the history of fashion.

Throughout the 50 plus years since the Gallery of English Costume in Manchester began to publish short picture-book catalogues of its collections, many other museums have followed this route. In part it was a response to the educational needs of pre-university level students with whom 'the costume project' became increasingly popular. Journalists applied their expertise to the subject, most notably Alison Adburgham, Ernestine Carter and Prudence Glynn in the United Kingdom. Adburgham's work, notably *Women in Print* (1972) and *Shopping in Style* (1979) opened up fruitful new areas, which have subsequently been expanded by successive generations of writers. The art historian Anne Hollander's *Seeing Through Clothes* (1975) and the fashion historian Valerie Steele's *Fashion and Eroticism: Ideals of Feminine Beauty from the Victorian Era to the Jazz Age* (1985) introduced new ways of considering the relationship between the body, clothing, gender and social conventions. Rozsika Parker, a feminist art historian, examined how and why embroidery diminished from an art form created by both sexes in the Middle Ages into a minor female craft in the post-1700 period before being revived in the 20th century. *The Subversive Stitch, Embroidery and the Making of the Feminine* (1984) is a social history of the changing relationships between women and embroidery and complements specialist books which analyze the history of embroidery techniques.

Running alongside these changing and far from 'internalized' approaches, which reflected new research and were written in clear and unambiguous language, were a growing number of books by costume curators and a small number of academic dress historians. They repositioned periods, themes and topics in line with new research but did not reflect an overtly feminist, political or theoretical agenda. Anne Buck, Stella Newton, Diana de Marly, Aileen Ribeiro, Penelope Byrde, Christina Walkley, Vanda Foster, Sarah

13. (above) A page from the 'Rossendale Collection' pattern book c. 1820

Samples of cotton calico are printed with one colour (or a resist) by roller and completed with further colours added by block. The printer was able to extend the range of patterns offered by creating many variations of striping and colouring for each engraved roller. A clever use of a limited range of fast colours gave the impression of a much wider range; for instance, by overprinting yellow on top of blue the greens on these patterns are formed.

The Rossendale Collection contains pattern books from 1808 to 1871 held by the Rossendale Design Studio. These books were gathered from various Lancashire mills, including the Loveclough print works operated by the Rossendale Printing Company. Surviving collections such as this one offer opportunities for collaboration between textile historians and dress curators.

14. (left) Woman's day dress c. 1825; photograph by John Chase

Cotton, with block- or roller-printed vertical serpentine lines in three colours, this dress has a high-waisted bodice attached to the back of the skirt and opens at the centre-front. The sleeves taper from fullness at the upper arm to the wrist, with a band and flare over the hand. The skirt has an apron front and gathering tapes, with five pleats at either side of the centre back to shape the skirt, and a loose straight belt; hand-sewn.

The description given above could be lengthened with details about measurements, how the garment was acquired, if it has undergone conservation, when it was exhibited, if it has been published, where similar garments in other collections can be found or if the design of the print can be identified (see Fig. 11). This is sometimes referred to as 'hemline history', an accumulation of details that are perceived to be associated with the history of dressmaking rather than cultural or social history. Similar criticisms are rarely made about detailed descriptions of ceramics, furniture, metalwork and painting. Curators of dress use this information as a means of identifying a garment, not as an end in itself, but theoreticians frequently overlook this, as although they seem fascinated by dress and its bodily associations they are repelled by, or dismissive of, surviving examples.

Levitt and others provided lucid and informative texts on a wide range of subject matter. Their source material ranged from archives to surviving dress. They wrote about economic, social and technical changes, patterns of consumption, about male and female dress, and their audience was the intelligent reader from every background, not just art historians, theatre designers or curators. This was work far superior to '...the easy pickings of literary quotation or ... amateur psychology'.

The 'cultural construction of the embodied identity'[11]

In the United Kingdom in 2002, there were over 500 colleges and universities whose syllabuses include fashion and its history as an option within, or as the focus of, a complete BA or MA course. These academic courses, ranging from the practical to the theoretical, are often cross-disciplinary in approach. Aspects of design and cultural history, gender studies, literary theory and sociology are woven into studies of how dress and the body are perceived, analyzed and interpreted. Students visit museums, some undertake placements within them, but there are fewer opportunities to pursue careers in this area than in the burgeoning universities, thus maintaining a divide, a sense of two cultures, of the old and new dress histories.

Tracing the development of the new dress history is problematic. Does it begin with Anne Hollander's *Seeing Through Clothes* (1975), Alison Lurie's *The Language of Clothes* (1981) or Elizabeth Wilson's *Adorned in Dreams* (1985), or with the exhibition *Men and Women, Dressing the Part* (1989) and accompanying volume of essays edited by Claudia Kidwell and Valerie Steele? Certainly the 1980s saw the first exploratory period of repositioning the study of dress/fashion within a number of theoretical frameworks. A useful starting place, because it looks both back at previous work and forwards, is Jennifer Craik's book *The Face of Fashion* (1994). In the preface she showed refreshing honesty when she offered her approach as '...starting points for students of fashion to expand, revise and embellish' once they had absorbed her '...interdisciplinary perspective, incorporating cultural studies, anthropology, sociology, art history and social history'.[12] In her introductory chapter Craik grouped and summarized her perception of the changes that had occurred since the late 1960s. She described certain historians of traditional dress history, selectively read as her bibliography indicates, such as the Cunningtons, Laver, Diana de Marly, Stella Newton and Colin McDowell as being narrow in their concerns. She accepted that Anne Hollander and Valerie Steele were 'rather more insightful and imaginative', but dismissed books devoted to the works of individual designers as 'eulogistic'.[13] Craik mentioned authors who had used psychological, sociological and anthropological perspectives, some from a much earlier period of dress studies such as Flügel and Veblen, and also considered those interdisciplinary studies that had been informed by literary criticism and new philosophical ideas, such as works by Roland Barthes, Elizabeth Wilson, Marjorie Garber, Jane Gaines and Charlotte Herzog. None, she felt, had grasped the complexity of the subject. *The Face of Fashion* is an interesting book, repositioning fashion within media studies and patterns of international consumption, and its ideas do not deter the reader by being shrouded in linguistic contortions. However she, like many writers, found it difficult to accommodate the work of other authors with different agendas to hers.

The Calico Printer.

15. 'The Calico Printer', an illustration from The Book of English Trades, *1823*
This depiction of block printing of calico presents a somewhat idealized image of craftsmanship with fresh air, methodical activity and a neatly dressed worker. The reality would have been much harsher in terms of hours worked and the demands made by employers.

16. 'The Tailor', an illustration from The Book of English Trades, 1823

The master tailor is carefully if not fashionably dressed; by this date many men wore trousers in preference to breeches. The apprentices who work for him are seated close to the windows of a room at the top of the shop/house where the light is at its best for hand sewing. This and the previous image are idealized propaganda for trades that became increasingly mechanized in the 19th century, demanded long hours and were not well paid. Work by economic historians which investigates production and not just consumption of the processes involved in the clothing trades is of use to dress historians.

Writing at that time, the early to mid 1990s, Craik was at the start of an almost industrial outpouring of books on dress, the body and appearance that reflected feminist, postmodernist or linguistic agendas. Omitted from this particular loop, although other authors cite them occasionally, are influential works by economic and social historians, including Beverly Lemire, Daniel Roche and Margaret Spufford. To Craik their kind of research was too narrow because it suggested that '...fashion is specific to capitalist economies, political practices and cultural formations'.[14] She seems not to have read Roche or she might have been sympathetic to his view that '...clothing is a good indicator of the material culture of a society, for it introduces us immediately to consumer patterns, and enables us to consider the social hierarchy of appearances'.[15] This idea is not dissimilar to Craik's acceptance that '...fashion relates to particular codes of behaviour and rules of ceremony and place'.[16] In 1995, Manchester University published Christopher Breward's *The Culture of Fashion. A New History of Fashionable Dress* within a series on Studies in Design and Material Culture. Unlike other authors he covered a longer time-span, from the Middle Ages onwards, with the intention of showing how the new critical approaches could be enhanced by a judicious interweaving of established and new methods. He used the work of traditional dress historians to discuss stylistic changes and then reassessed the evidence in the context of complementary analyses. In the words of Elizabeth Wilson: 'The author introduces the reader to considerations of class, gender, economic and symbolic meanings in a clear and attractive way. At last the new fashion scholarship is established in an accessible form, in a text which recognizes the complex ways in which fashions are generated and also the varied methodologies we need to study them'.[17] Intentionally he did not discuss the role of collections of surviving dress and used photographs of such material selectively, principally as examples of changes in construction or the use of fabrics. He tended to make the same assumption as other modern writers that a book by a traditional dress historian is all that they ever publish, overlooking the articles, catalogue entries and essays they may have produced. However, on the whole, cultural historians, though comfortable with theoretical writing, tend to be more well read in traditional dress history and less dismissive of it than some practitioners from other disciplines.

One of the most notable developments in publications containing new approaches to dress history is the fragmentary nature of their composition. Joint authorships or edited compilations of essays that result from a conference or an informal association between scholars with similar or allied research interests, are published almost as regularly as learned journals. One result of this is that the essays are of uneven standard; the book has replaced the journal as a forum of inclusivity, offering unproven authors equality of space and opportunity alongside their more experienced colleagues. Before the academic publishing boom of the 1990s, there was an informal route for new authors. They reviewed books, learned how to write coherently and thoughtfully, and applied this experience to longer articles or essays. Eventually, these skills might be used in writing a book. The old system crumbled under the weight of many more postgraduate courses and doctoral theses. A postgraduate student who has spent two to five years researching, offering papers at numerous seminars and conferences worldwide which culminate in a doctoral thesis of 90,000 words or more, is likely to believe that the apprenticeship has been served. In most cases, the real apprenticeship is just beginning.

18. Man's evening waistcoat, fabric detail c. 1838–43
This waistcoat was made from figured silk velvet with deep crimson pile on a bright blue ground, with buttons covered in the same fabric. The diversity of colours and fabrics offered a bold contrast to the plainer coats and trousers of the late 1830s and early 1840s.

17. Man's waistcoat c. 1840; photograph by John Chase
The waistcoat is created from wool embroidery on canvas lined and backed with white cotton and linen, hand-sewn. The adjustment band at the back of the waistcoat contains four rows of elastic, which was beginning to be used for clothes and accessories from the 1830s onwards. This type of brightly coloured embroidery was called Berlin wool work after its German origins and was immensely popular throughout much of the century, though relatively uncreative. The marked canvas and wools could be bought in shops throughout Europe and America. Waistcoats, slippers, pictures, cushions, chair covers and much more survive in quantity. The obsessive nature of such work was recorded in a poem of 1852, in which a husband laments that his wife is always engaged in such work and even when visitors arrive:

'She stares too at the gentleman, and when I ask her why,
'Tis "Oh my love, the pattern of his waistcoat struck my eye".'

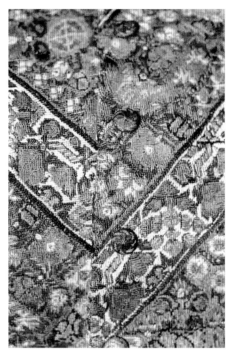

19. Man's waistcoat, fabric detail c. 1840–43
The horizontal bands embroidered in multi-coloured silks are thought to be from an Iranian or Turkish textile. This and the two previous waistcoats are just a small sample of the many patterned and brightly coloured men's waistcoats that survive in museum collections. The evolution of the waistcoat, its changing role, shape, decoration and ultimate disappearance as an essential part of formal male dress, is an interesting topic because it existed alongside and often in contrast to the coat and breeches/trousers.

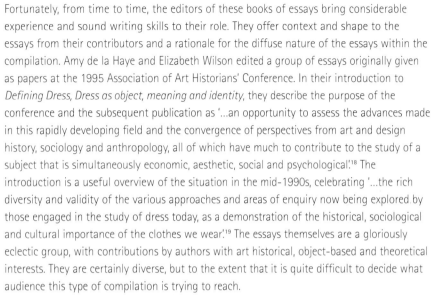

Fortunately, from time to time, the editors of these books of essays bring considerable experience and sound writing skills to their role. They offer context and shape to the essays from their contributors and a rationale for the diffuse nature of the essays within the compilation. Amy de la Haye and Elizabeth Wilson edited a group of essays originally given as papers at the 1995 Association of Art Historians' Conference. In their introduction to *Defining Dress, Dress as object, meaning and identity*, they describe the purpose of the conference and the subsequent publication as '...an opportunity to assess the advances made in this rapidly developing field and the convergence of perspectives from art and design history, sociology and anthropology, all of which have much to contribute to the study of a subject that is simultaneously economic, aesthetic, social and psychological'.[18] The introduction is a useful overview of the situation in the mid-1990s, celebrating '...the rich diversity and validity of the various approaches and areas of enquiry now being explored by those engaged in the study of dress today, as a demonstration of the historical, sociological and cultural importance of the clothes we wear'.[19] The essays themselves are a gloriously eclectic group, with contributions by authors with art historical, object-based and theoretical interests. They are certainly diverse, but to the extent that it is quite difficult to decide what audience this type of compilation is trying to reach.

The arrival of a new journal, as we have seen earlier, can be a sign that a subject area is becoming established. Therefore it was significant when, in 1996, Berg, an imprint of the New York University Press with a British office in Oxford, launched a new quarterly journal: *Fashion Theory, The Journal of Dress, Body & Culture*. Their editorial board decided that fashion could be defined '...as the cultural construction of an embodied identity...' and, in the dismissive way of the new dress history, stated that '...the study of fashion has, until recently, suffered from a lack of critical analysis'[20] In its *Dress, Body, Culture* series of books, Berg has published extensively in the last few years. They publish many edited collections of essays alongside single-author books and their subject matter is both cross-disciplinary and worldwide in scope. In 2002 they announced a new journal named *Textile: The Journal of Cloth & Culture*, and a new series of books entitled *Textiles That Changed the World*. The journal, described as 'multidisciplinary', invites articles 'informed by technology and visual media, history and cultural theory, anthropology, philosophy, political economy and psychoanalysis', thereby complementing *Fashion Theory*, which invites submissions across a similar range. This is very shrewd product positioning; both journals are aimed at established or new academics who have to publish to maintain and enhance their careers. In turn they will ensure that their college libraries order these publications and their students read them. Like all journals, the content of *Fashion Theory* is uneven but it does provide evidence of the varying approaches and disciplines now concerned with all aspects of appearance and not just clothing.

Fashioning the Frame, Boundaries, Dress and the Body, one of Berg's many books was published in 1998. Its authors, Warwick and Cavallaro, are academics in universities and engaged in the new interdisciplinary dress history, principally from the perspective of modern literary criticism. They wrote: 'Many fashion historians seem to subscribe to Laver's tripartite mapping out of the possible motivations lying behind the wearing of garments...' and then described Laver's Utility, Hierarchical and Seduction Principles as an 'influential theory'.[21] They appear to have read Laver's *Taste and Fashion* (1937) and his *Modesty in Dress* (1969) but they cite few other dress historians in their bibliography or text so this idea of 'many fashion historians' subscribing to Laver's views is unproven. This would hardly matter if Laver's books, useful in many respects (not least their admirable range of illustrations) were not still a feature of university or other library collections, which should have acquired more recent publications of the type mentioned in the earlier section of this chapter (see pages 36, 38–39). However, Warwick and Cavallaro do provide a complex and wide-ranging series of essays, which offer a snapshot of the iconic writers admired and referred to by many practitioners of the new dress history: Barthes, Baudrillard, Derrida, Foucault, Kristeva and Lacan. Individually or together these practitioners assist entry into the fields of literary theory, philosophy and psychoanalytic criticism and the worlds of postmodernism, structuralism and post-structuralism. This is immensely difficult terrain but it is an instructive example of the new dress history at its most linguistically impenetrable.

Academics have always written for their peer group, but rarely with such dependence upon the theories of others and such selective reading within the traditional fashion histories they criticize. Those excluded from this world – students starting out, curious general readers, curators of collections in which dress and textiles reside – lack strong, intelligible, well-written texts that actually assist their understanding of this new discipline. Michael Carter's book *Fashion Classics* (see page 34) would have been even more useful if he had offered some entry points into these new areas. It is short-sighted of established academics who profess interest in the subject of dress/fashion, however widely or narrowly drawn, to demonstrate an unwillingness to engage with the breadth of the discipline and its history of language clarity. They are well placed to demand clear analysis and description unfogged by concepts that distance their work from all but a small committed audience of their peers. This can be seen all too frequently when such authors do venture into the terminology of dress and make risible mistakes, such as confusing blouses with men's shirts in the 16th century and crinolines for hoops in the 18th, or make pronouncements that they falsely perceive to be original because they are not widely enough read.

Material Strategies, Dress and Gender in Historical Perspective, edited by Barbara Burman and Carole Turbin, is a more recent and much more accessible book of essays. They examine changes in the discipline in the last 25 years or so, and pinpoint how scholars have omitted '...to systematically analyze dress and visual material culture'.[22] They offer the view that until the early 1980s '...the study of dress in the West was largely dominated by costume historians, collectors, art historians and museum curators who contributed a rich though limited body of knowledge and detailed visual record of continual changes in garment styles and textiles'.[23] The limitations they identify are that such work concentrated on the clothing of elite groups and was principally connoisseurial, though leavened by judicious application of Veblen's theories about conspicuous consumption. In the early 1980s a '...more analytical approach to dress within visual and material culture...' appeared as a result of new studies in consumption across all levels in society.[24] In revisiting the evolution of dress history studies, from the early 20th-century narrative chronologies of elite styles of Western clothing up to the present day, we encounter the idea that, in the words of Burman and Turbin, 'fashion and textile history is still in transition'. Having noted

20. The Orphan Milliners, *magazine illustration from 1844*

Young women, including orphans from country areas as in this engraving, were taught fine sewing and sent to make a living in the businesses of fashionable dressmakers' shops. The sweatshop conditions and poor pay were often ruinous to their health. They are depicted working at 12:55am, finishing an evening dress under the forbidding gaze of the workroom supervisor.

One of the reasons behind collections of costume being considered unrepresentative is that they contain so many examples of the clothing worn by elite groups in society. However, presenting such garments within the context of the processes of production and consumption is now an accepted feature of discussion within museum displays and educational work as well as in articles and books.

that the discipline is no longer the preserve of journalists, art and costume historians, they explain what they perceive to be occurring:

'Scholars from diverse fields and perspectives have opened up fashion history to consider dress as central to visual and material culture for people worldwide. They seek to understand the complex influences of consumption and production and their interstices, explore the gendered dimensions of national identity and develop new ways of looking at the relationship between public and private life, the body and sexuality.'[25]

Both this approach and that of de la Haye and Wilson, mentioned earlier, are admirable up to a point. What they do not consider is the fact that a much wider audience is interested and personally engaged with how dress is presented to them in any form: garments, illustration, mementos, photographs, film and video. The non-academic, non-specialist public are the audience for and the critics of how their money is spent directly or indirectly: on museums, historic buildings, special exhibitions, the theatre, the cinema, television, books and universities. If the academic world is setting the agenda for how dress is interpreted they should have regard for the needs of this wider public and its willingness, or not, to be persuaded by complex ideas. We can still read James Laver or François Boucher and even if we find them dated, elitist and patriarchal in their views, the words are not mystifying and offer us a coherent text within which to evaluate and interpolate new approaches. The apparent willingness to discard the history of the subject and, more especially, the way in which collections of dress, invariably described as 'costume' (now obviously a pejorative term), were assembled and studied is unnecessary. Writing about costume/dress/fashion should celebrate the fact that it is a subject of study and that earlier studies inform us about the differing but valid perceptions and interpretations throughout the subject's evolution.

Finding a route through the maze of new publications on appearance, the body and dress/fashion is a Herculean task, and this cannot be more than a sketchy introduction to its complexities. The important thing is to stand back and try to consider how and why something as ephemeral as fashion and appearance has generated so much academic attention. Is it a passing phase, the equivalent of the pursuit of the sublime, neoclassicism, romanticism or existentialism? Fashion has, throughout its long history, spawned successive new forms of production, manufacture and consumption – and the latest is the theorizing business. Within this there are undoubtedly interesting challenges to ideas from previous generations of writers, but identifying what is significant in this new work and what is peripheral is far from easy.

As a beginner's guide through this jungle of theory I have provided an appendix to this book that, for the reader unfamiliar with either the iconic authors or the movements with which they are associated, offers some information in the clearest language possible given the complexity of some of the subject matter. One of the major difficulties in defining the new dress history is that it has been annexed or subsumed into other disciplines – anthropology, cultural history, literature, to name some of the most obvious – but it has also been re-examined in the light of movements such as feminism and postmodernism. Naturally this is refreshing, as subjects die when they do not find new interest and expression from outside; introversion leads to atrophy. Decisions about what names and movements to include in the appendix have been determined by how frequently these are mentioned in new or recently published articles, essays and books. Some names and movements are common to several disciplines, others are more clearly allied to authors whose area of interest is defined as art history, cultural history, design history, feminist history, gender studies, literary criticism, social anthropology, sociology or just history. The interdisciplinary nature of modern scholarship can mislead the unwary reader. For example, if Roland Barthes and Michel Foucault are cited, this might indicate linguistic and philosophical interests but this is not so – both are considered seminal authors and quoted by a wide range of authors who might have other agendas. Walter Benjamin and Theodor Adorno are Frankfurt School philosophers whose principal impact could be on other philosophers, social anthropologists and sociologists, but art and cultural historians also cite them. Feminist historians cite Simone de Beauvoir, Elizabeth Wilson, Jennifer Craik and Marjorie Garber but also Barthes and Foucault. This cross-fertilization of disciplines and sources should be illuminating but its principal legacy is its ability to confuse and deter readers, a state of affairs wholly at variance with the contemporary notion that information should be readily accessible. Obviously there are hierarchies of information in all disciplines, from very easy to very difficult, but outside of children's books, it is rare to find guidance on what pre-knowledge (or reading age) is required before purchase. However, it would be disconcerting if all these books were lumped together as too difficult and the most useful and clearly written did not reach a wider audience. This is an issue that publishers should consider as and when they commission new authors and titles.

The academic and museum-based traditions have blended from time to time, but usually only in regard to modern subjects, such as the 1994–5 exhibition at the Victoria & Albert Museum in London: StreetStyle: From Sidewalk to Catwalk, 1940 to Tomorrow. Cultural commentaries also accompany more widely drawn exhibitions in which fashion plays an interesting role through a complex web of references to performance and installation art, film, photography and video. All writers on dress/fashion have been influenced, to a greater or lesser extent, by the preoccupations of the last quarter of a century, but maintaining an even-handed approach to writing about the subject is far from easy. Relationships between publishers and academic institutions have been fostered in a way that leaves authors at a disadvantage. Large museums often have publishing programmes and produce important additions to the literature on how garments can be used and analyzed, the Victoria & Albert Museum's excellent series on *Dress in Detail* being an obvious example. However, most curators have limited time for research and writing; there are no sabbaticals and few opportunities for visiting lectureships or fellowships. This means that those knowledgeable about collections and their links to themes of consumption, production and how the interpretation of material culture can stand alongside or interlock with modern theories, find it increasingly difficult to compete with their colleagues in universities.

3 Collecting dress

"Collection: group of things collected and belonging together (literary materials, specimens, fashionable clothes, works of art, etc.)' Concise Oxford Dictionary[1]

'... we use categorising and organising everywhere in our lives – in the library, in the supermarket, even – perhaps in (our) own wardrobe!' British Museum leaflet[2]

We are surrounded by public and private collections, painstakingly assembled to provide a three-dimensional 'library' of the impact of design, technical change and social customs on styles of dress and textiles. We take for granted that we have almost limitless opportunities to visit museums and enjoy special exhibitions that deal specifically or tangentially with both the dress of the past and contemporary fashion. Today public collecting is informed by carefully written policies, of a local, regional, national or international dimension, which define the kind of pieces that museums will collect and those that will be regretfully refused. However, the enthusiasm of past individuals and institutions means that the sheer quantity of surviving dress, textiles and accessories is immense. In the heyday of collecting and museum expansion this was seen as advantageous: large collections, given that costume is fragile and light-sensitive, meant that regular rotational needs could be met, and that there would be reserves of material for research and study purposes.

The history of collecting has a long and distinguished pedigree but the collecting of dress (rather than textiles) is a relatively recent phenomenon and is the subject of this chapter. In considering that process, with examples drawn from both public and private spheres, it is possible to see how and why it took so long for dress to be considered an acceptable area of study. It is always useful when undertaking research into museum collections to find out when and why groups or individual artefacts entered a collection and from what source. Such information can offer evidence about changing reasons for collecting and the artistic and social attitudes that underpinned these reasons.

Public and private: early collecting

The desire to collect a 'group of things', using the dictionary definition at the head of this chapter, can be traced much further back than the late 17th century, but was given momentum by the increased opportunity to travel and trade throughout the known world from the second half of that century onwards. Trading links provided a means by which not only goods, but also unusual customs and different civilizations were discovered. Cabinets of curiosities were assembled, one of the most influential of which in 17th-century England was that owned by the Tradescant family. It was acquired by Elias Ashmole and eventually became the Ashmolean Museum in Oxford, which opened in 1683. Although the term 'curiosity' has, to modern sensibilities, a quaint or pejorative sound, it merely means a strange or rare object. The desire not only to acquire interesting items from around the known world, but also to list and exhibit them is more noticeable from the 16th century onwards. These groups of curiosities included articles of clothing and accessories, which demonstrates a complex set of interests – in place, craftsmanship, materials and people. The idea of collecting artefacts from different cultures as a primitive means of examination and classification was evolving. In certain instances this led to the development of museums with collections that range widely across cultures and continents, such as the Ashmolean, the British Museum in London, founded in 1753, and the Rijksmuseum in Amsterdam, originally founded in 1808 as a gallery of Dutch art but which gradually expanded to encompass Dutch history, sculpture, prints, lace, oriental art and costume. Later still, other museums dealing with specific subject matter – a place, a discipline, a person, for example – developed alongside the more broadly based institutions.

The educational significance of such collections was usually an element in their assembly and arrangement, but there was also another aspect, less easy to grasp today, which is that of the public show. If you knew nothing of Native American Indians and had no idea of where North America was, the sight of a moccasin was both fascinating and strange – a symbol of a culture wholly unknown, probably unimagined. Such early collections were wide-ranging in their curiosity and have, in subsequent centuries, been added to, analyzed and written about. Catalogues of such collections provide useful evidence of what was collected: the origins of each artefact, with its date if known, which was sometimes rather loosely assessed (glove, 17th century is not much use as a date); methods of construction and use of fabric; details of provenance, meaning its first owner and its line of descent to the present day. *Tradescant's Rarities*, the catalogue of the earliest group within the Ashmolean Museum, was published in 1983 to mark the museum's tercentenary. It provides a series of essays on the background of the collection, and on the history of collecting in Europe as a context within which the Tradescants' interests and achievement can be assessed. It is divided into sections according to continent, with detailed descriptions of each item either accompanied by line drawings or photographs. The entries were written by scholars and curators who knew their subject area well, but anyone interested in the clothing and accessories, which include a rare late-17th-century Native American skin shirt, footwear from various continents, gloves and jewellery, will not find them grouped together but spread between continents.

Not all 17th-century collections demonstrated the range of scientific and anthropological content found in the early Ashmolean Museum; others were either more limited or more personal in content and range. Possessions were a significant form of wealth in the pre-banking period and for many years after such institutions were founded. Inventories of personal effects often list clothing and domestic textiles, and cover many different social groups, from elite members of society to artisans. Clothing, however, unless it had a family significance and the family was wealthy enough not to dispose of it, rarely survived. The Verney family of Claydon in Buckinghamshire, England, provide an example of contextualized survivals of clothing from the 17th century. Their house, now administered by the National Trust but still occupied by the Verney family, presents a pleasing microcosm of changing tastes in architecture, interior decoration and collecting over nearly three centuries. Tucked away in a display case is a faded but still magnificent court suit worn for the coronation of

21. (left) Venetian Gros Point lace collar c. 1660; photograph by John Chase
This linen collar with a pattern of flowers and leaves is needle lace, a feature of which is its almost three-dimensional quality. Italian lace was expensive but popular in the late 17th century. In portraits there are many examples of such collars before linen cravats edged with bobbin lace replaced them.

22. (below) Venetian Rose Point lace c. 1660
The dealer's label gives a stock number 2404 and a price of 25/- (£1.25) for this piece. Lace was removed from clothing and usually laundered separately. In the late 17th century this painstaking process could take up to three days and reflected the monetary and social value of such pieces. Lace, like embroidery and tapestry, was admired for its design and craft skills; its survival in considerable quantities was considered instructional as well as aesthetic.

Charles II in 1661. Such a garment is a rare survival, but there are other garments, both earlier and later. Why do they survive? This is the conundrum of all surviving dress: why keep something that could be cut up and used for children's clothing, made into cushions, pawned or sold on the thriving second-hand market in London? There is no obvious answer except for the one we might all understand. 'Best clothes', or more accurately clothes for special events, are often kept as they retain a heightened significance. Some modern scholars have called them 'the materials of memory', which suggests they are more than clothing, suffused with a relevance, a bodily recollection that transforms garments into ritualistic relics of an individual, a time and an event.[3] This is an idea not wholly appropriate to pragmatic 17th-century attitudes towards clothing but, for whatever reason, the clothes were put away, forgotten, and not altered for fancy dress in later centuries.

The Verneys are interesting for much more than the surviving clothing they retained; they were assiduous letter writers, kept detailed accounts and, in every sense, appear to have been instinctive collectors of their own history. However, survivals of clothing from the 17th century are rare; there are enough complete and incomplete garments from the pre- and post-Civil War period to offer limited evidence of style, construction, decoration and selection and use of fabric, but they are scattered between a number of public and

23. Sampler, English c. 1660-80 (detail)

The linen is embroidered in silk in a variety of stitches; two raised-work snakes are located above a woman in a dress of raised buttonhole stitch decorated with beads and seed pearls in a garden with flowers and insects. A set of upper-case alphabet letters and the name MARY TOVEY are embroidered at the base of the sampler.

Samplers were practice pieces for girls who, if their embroidery skills were good enough, might progress to cushions, needlework caskets, beadwork trays or mirror surrounds. There are many examples of 17th-century embroideries in museum collections of varying degrees of proficiency, but with a fairly narrow range of subject matter. Skilful copying is more noticeable than originality. Pieces like this are now being recontextualized to assess the needlework skills that women acquired across several centuries and how such skills could be used to earn a living rather than just provide a domestic accomplishment.

private collections. Not until quite recently has there been an attempt to list all of the 17th-century clothing in the United Kingdom, an exercise being undertaken by Professor Aileen Ribeiro of the Courtauld Institute of Art for a book on the dress of this period.

There is certainly nothing in the United Kingdom to match the important European collections in Sweden and Denmark, which contain 17th-century garments that were kept because they had been worn by rulers, their consorts and their family members on significant occasions. This is clothing with secure provenance; admittedly it is atypical in that it was worn for highly rarefied events such as coronations, weddings and so forth, but in construction and style it is wholly in keeping with mainstream developments in fashion and the textiles used for dress. In England, although John Tradescant had worked for Charles I, there is nothing in his collection of the significance of the royal garments in the Danish and Swedish Royal Armouries. In 1989 an exhibition, Royal Treasures of Sweden 1550–1700, previously seen in America, was held at the Royal Academy of Arts in London. The accompanying illustrated catalogue gave detailed descriptions of surviving royal dress from the early to mid-17th century. The fabrics, colours and construction demonstrate the international nature of fashionable men's clothing in western Europe at this time. Although this catalogue contains only a selection of surviving dress from the Swedish collections, it is indicative of what might have been saved if a similar approach to collecting had been attempted in England, if only after the Restoration in 1660.

Obviously dress did survive, otherwise there would be no 17th-century examples in modern museum collections, but with a few notable exceptions (the Isham collection at the Victoria & Albert Museum in London, for example), it has no provenance, had been bought abroad, overlooked in attics or found and retained by artists for whom it was a useful studio prop. If a royal collection similar to those in Denmark and Sweden had been formed in England it would probably have included such garments as the suit worn by James II when, as Duke of York, he married his second wife Princess Mary of Modena in 1673. This was retained in the de Sausmarez family on the Isle of Guernsey until it was bought by the Victoria & Albert Museum in 1992. Little associated with Charles II survives apart from the Garter clothes worn on the effigy carried in his funeral procession in 1685 and kept with a number of effigies in the Westminster Abbey museum. Much more survives to record the appearance and clothing of Peter the Great of Russia (reigned 1682–1725) and his successors, and this despite the revolution of 1917. Certainly the Hanoverian dynasty, twice threatened by invasions on behalf of Stuart pretenders to the throne, had little reason to retain clothing worn by the Stuart monarchs, but neither did they attempt to record their own dynasty in this way until the reign of Queen Victoria. It was often private collectors who acquired such relics as did survive and an interesting discussion of two collectors, Ralph Thoresby in the late 17th century and Horace Walpole in the 18th century, and their successive ownership of a pair of James I & VI's gloves, is found in an article in *Costume* in 1990.[4]

After the foundation of the British Museum in 1753 there was a hiatus in public museum development until the early to mid-19th century. The British Museum has never established a department of dress and textiles, preferring to arrange their collections by period or category, so that ethnographic dress, textiles and jewellery are kept separate from those of early Egypt, and the Schreiber collection of fans is kept with prints and drawings. Something of the museum's view of this type of material is captured in the quotation at the head of this chapter, which comes from the children's guide to the Enlightenment galleries. It suggests that the wardrobe, and by inference clothing, is a less significant area of categorization than the supermarket shelf. In the age of the Enlightenment, however, private collecting continued unabated, and local antiquarian and philosophical societies assembled a variety of artefacts, usually of anthropological or archaeological significance. However, the collecting of past and contemporary European clothing played little part in these early initiatives. Collecting dress was a fairly informal affair. Artists who specialized in history painting sought out fabrics and garments that might be useful in their work, some of them accruing substantial collections. Theatre wardrobes also benefited from purchases or gifts: the actor–manager Tate Wilkinson's *Memoirs*, published in 1790, offer insights into the theatrical transformation of garments, which had '...at different periods of time, bedecked real lords and dukes, and were bought at much less price than now...'.[5] Later, as public collections were established, there were numerous donations and some sales from both professional and amateur theatrical wardrobes to museums. The problematical nature of such gifts is highlighted by Tate

Collecting dress

Wilkinson's comments and they continue to pose intriguing problems to modern curators, more especially when the early origins of such donations are uncertain.

In the sphere of private collections that eventually found their way into museums, many types of useful evidence complement actual garments. Barbara Johnson's album, which recorded her interest in the world of fashion from the precocious age of eight in 1746 up to 1823, two years before her death, provides an insight into an individual's taste in styles, fabrics and fashion illustration. The album contains fabric samples, details about quantities and the final garment as it was made up. It was acquired by the Victoria & Albert Museum and published in facsimile in 1987. This invaluable resource for students and scholars of 18th-century dress can be supplemented by viewing another collection, the dolls dressed by Laetitia Clark Powell. She chose a different method of recording her tastes in dress to that adopted by Barbara Johnson: her dolls wear miniature versions of her favourite clothes. The earliest is dated 1754, and other members of the family maintained the tradition until 1911. When this exceptional group was donated to Bethnal Green Museum (now the Museum of Childhood) each doll was found to have a label with the date when the doll was dressed, and some have a brief description of the garments. This was a domestic and highly personal version of the fashion doll.

Fashion dolls wore miniature examples of the latest fashions and, from the late medieval period onwards, were a favourite way of disseminating the latest information on fabric, colour, cut and decoration. Some survive in museum collections: Lord and Lady Clapham, c.1690–1700 in the Victoria & Albert Museum, are a rare early pair, but the majority date from the 18th century. Fashion dolls overlapped for some considerable time with printed illustrations of the latest fashions and collections of these were assembled from the late 17th century onwards, John Evelyn and Samuel Pepys both collecting the early French examples. The print was gradually replaced by the photograph from the late 1830s, although fashion illustration and sketches by designers continued the long tradition of drawing for recollection and to capture ideas, and this type of material gradually found its way into museum collections. Early museums had relatively few staff and did not operate as carefully as do modern museums with regard to the storage of collections and deciding where the responsibility for them lay. This was beneficial because consideration of relationships between different types of collection and the information they contain allows the curator, student or researcher endless scope for making useful connections in regard to visual and written evidence and the processes of production.

A published précis of this proliferation of potential source material is given in Janet Arnold's *A Handbook of Costume*. This was devised as a guide to students in the early 1970s and her list of primary sources covers twelve sections: paintings; sculpture (including ivory and wood carvings, monumental effigies etc.); graphic arts (including drawings, engravings, woodcuts, fashion plates, caricatures and book illustrations); manuscript illuminations and portrait miniatures; wall paintings, frescoes, mosaics and stained glass; monumental brasses; silhouettes, daguerreotypes, photographs and films; ceramics, glass, coins, medals and other objects that use costumed figures for decoration; dolls; tapestries, embroidery, printed and woven textiles; archive material, literary sources, periodicals and newspapers; patterns and technical works on tailoring and dressmaking.[6]

24. Lord and Lady Clapham, English 1690–1700
This pair of fashionably dressed dolls have the faces of children's playthings and the wardrobe of sophisticated adults. They are layered, from miniature underclothing to the accessories like shoes and headwear. Their importance is not merely that they survive as a pair but that they offer a microcosmic view of how a complete set of male and female clothes of the 1690s were made and worn.
(By courtesy, V&A Picture Library)

This is a formidable range even before the reader encounters the actual collections of dress; the latter take up approximately one third of the book. The intriguing thing about the list of primary sources is its hierarchical nature, apparently following an art-historical view of the primacy of certain categories over others; it would have been equally reasonable to have followed an alphabetical listing with 'archive material' coming first and 'wall paintings' last of all. However, the point she made is as pertinent now as in the 1970s: almost anything collected by a museum, art gallery, record office or specialist library can and does add to understanding of the dress of the past. The reason why the list has been given such prominence here is that a great many of the categories were collected long before the serious collecting of dress took place in museums.

Forming public collections of dress 1850–1970

In the 1830s the British government was fretting about the domination of the luxury goods market by French imports which, inevitably, included dress, fabrics and accessories. In 1835 a Select Committee of Arts and Manufactures was appointed to investigate 'the best means of extending a knowledge of the ARTS and the PRINCIPLES of DESIGN among the People (especially the Manufacturing Population) of the country; also to inquire into the constitution, management and effects of institutions concerned with the Arts'.[7] Unsurprisingly, when the Committee's recommendations were published they included the setting up of schools of design and the provision of more museums for educational

25. *Suit of coat and breeches worn by James, Duke of York, for the confirmation of his marriage contract to Princess Mary of Modena, 1673*
The suit is of heather-coloured wool, lined with red silk and embroidered with silver and silver-gilt thread. The coat bears the embroidered Star of the Order of the Garter on the left breast. The cravat and cuffs are of Venetian needle lace. This rare survival of a 17th-century Royal suit with an unimpeachable provenance owes nothing to the collecting instincts of the Stuarts or their successors, but to the simple fact that James gave the suit to one of his circle and it descended in their family until it was auctioned in 1992. It was bought by the Victoria & Albert Museum in London as an exceptional example of a dated man's suit of the transitional period between 1666 and 1676. This is public collecting at its most informed. (By courtesy, V&A Picture Library)

purposes. By 1837 a School of Design in Ornamental Art had been founded at Somerset House in London, but the Victoria & Albert Museum, the first of the new museums devoted to arts and manufacture, only opened in its original home at Marlborough House in 1852. Just three years later a bill was introduced in parliament, which authorized the establishment of 'Free Libraries and Museums in all large Towns'. Later in that year when the bill had been enforced the new law allowed municipal corporations to spend a penny rate on libraries and museums, but only after the new Act of Parliament had been adopted by a special poll of the ratepayers.[8] In 1850 there were probably fewer than 50 museums in the UK, most of which were privately financed and run by local philosophical and archaeological societies, but by the end of the century there were around 200. This ad hoc nature of provision was both enabling and disabling, as no strategy for collecting, care, research and display accompanied the rush to create museums that would educate and influence their visitors. Regional and local centres were, in principle, a good idea, but they unleashed the possibility of duplication, over-collecting and confusion about what a museum should offer its visitors.

Henry Cole, the first Director of the Victoria & Albert Museum, made a statement in 1863 about the purpose of his museum: 'The decorative art of all periods and all countries should be completely represented. Classic art ought not to be omitted, but inasmuch as the British Museum is particularly devoted to the illustration of classic art, it should be represented only to a limited extent'.[9] This conscious decision not to compete with the British Museum was both pragmatic and informed by the idea that there was no obvious public collection that met the needs of the 1835 Select Committee. In the aftermath of the considerable national and international acclaim for the Great Exhibition of 1851, there were so many gaps within the few museum displays open to the general public that a complementary approach offered considerable scope. There was, and remains, a distinct difference in their approach to collecting textiles and artefacts associated with human appearance. The Victoria & Albert Museum pioneered and led the field in the acquisition of, research into, and display of textiles and, somewhat later, fashionable dress.

During the early period of the Victoria & Albert Museum's existence the acquisition of dress was coincidental to that of acquiring textiles. The purpose of such material was to display fabrics and techniques rather than to present dress as either an artistic or social record. Their website is remarkably frank about the situation that once prevailed, stating that the museum '...has collected both textiles and dress since its earliest days. For many years garments were only acquired if they were made of significant textiles, as fashion had a low status within the decorative arts. The importance of fashion is now fully recognized and the Museum's collection of dress and accessories is of international importance'.[10] This 'low status' has bedevilled the subject and in the 1920s and early 1930s the Quennells listed only three public costume collections, and C W Cunnington, a dress historian rather than a general historian, could only list 19 in 1937.[11] The Victoria & Albert Museum appeared in both lists but was not admired by Cunnington, and a thoroughly professional approach to display and interpretation only occurred with the appointment of staff dedicated to the costume collection and the opening of a dedicated gallery, the Costume Court in 1962.

The principal problem was not the lack of popularity of displays of dress with the public.

It was more one of association: dress was ephemeral and intimate; it was perceived as something that could be cut up, remade, worn for fancy dress or, in hard times, pawned or sold. Somehow it had always missed being considered a significant or valuable record, unlike carpets, embroideries and tapestries. Where dress did survive, in a number of European collections and some that were evolving in North America, it was often treated as an adjunct to personal biography or national history. The great waxworks' shows presented historical figures in actual garments acquired from a deceased 'celebrity' – Madame de Pompadour, George IV or similar – offering the spectacle of a three-dimensional panorama of historical personalities. It was as if an history painting had acquired an extra dimension or a great theatrical production had frozen into a tableau for the delight of its audience. It was briefly amusing but the garments of the past, removed from the skill of a waxworks presentation or the bravura of stage performance, appeared lifeless and awkward. This did not prevent groups and individuals from collecting costume, and the movement to create large museums with educational aims and objectives, in capital cities or major regional towns, was international in nature from the late 19th century onwards. The examples given in this and the next chapter are selected because they identify both the strengths and weaknesses inherent in assembling large collections of dress. The museums are discussed in the order in which they were either founded or began to be closely associated with collections of dress and textiles.

The origins of the Rijksmuseum in Amsterdam can be found within three separate bodies: the Royal Cabinet of Curiosities, the Netherlands Museum of History and Art and the Royal Antiquarian Society. Each of these contained textiles that had been preserved as interesting curios or because they were closely linked to major personalities or events in the nation's history. However, it was the Royal Antiquarian Society that seemed to have most in common with the founders of the Victoria & Albert Museum in London. The Society was founded in 1858 in order to increase '...knowledge of Antiquities, in particular as sources for History, Art and Industry'.[12] Its members came from leading Amsterdam families and it collected with the aim of making the material available for study. By 1874 it was advocating a National Museum of Antiquities, which the Rijksmuseum in effect became. In the Hague, the Netherlands Museum of History and Art had been active in either buying or taking donations of costume and accessories, including examples of national costumes. Once the Rijksmuseum was established in its spacious new building in 1885, it took gifts or loans from the three bodies mentioned earlier. It also benefited from further collecting initiatives by interested directors or curators. In 1889 a room was opened in the Rijksmuseum to display textile art and items of dress from the various museums and societies. After the national costumes were transferred to the Open Air Museum at Arnhem in 1916 only fashionable dress from elite groups was collected, with an emphasis on the quality of the items, their historical significance and their provenance.[13]

The collection was systematically listed from 1920 and in 1923 a gallery was devoted to a chronological display complemented by portraits. A publication on the collection was produced in 1926. In *The Costumes of Our Ancestors 1700–1900*, 50 costumes, either photographed or drawn, were used as the basis for 12 chapters on the development of dress across two centuries. It also included patterns of five women's and two men's garments drawn to scale.[14] However, there was no professional curator until 1947 and although the collection grew there were no comprehensive displays until 1962. When they did appear, they were located in a series of specially designed period rooms, within which a chronological display was arranged.

It takes imagination and originality to break down deep-seated prejudices about what is worthy of acquisition and display, and this was found at the London Museum. In 1911, due to the vision of two energetic and well-connected minor peers, Lords Esher and Harcourt, it was suggested that London needed a museum about the Imperial capital to rival the Carnavalet in Paris, a museum devoted to the history of that city. There was no money, no building and no collections. Undeterred, they found a Keeper in the person of Guy Laking and the trio set about its apparently insurmountable task with shrewd wheeler-dealing and a keen eye for publicity. When the new museum opened to queues of potential visitors and a private visit by George V, Queen Mary and two of their children, barely a year had passed. In that time a skeleton staff had been appointed, temporary premises found in Kensington Palace and a collection of 18,000 artefacts assembled through a mixture of public appeals, assiduous courtship of benefactor-collectors, purchases and loans. From the outset, dress (not textiles) was a significant element in the new museum's collection. The history painter John Seymour Lucas's extensive collection of historic costume was being offered for sale and one of the interested parties was the Metropolitan Museum in New York. It was bought by the London Museum from under the noses of the established American museum, and at £1000, was less than the Metropolitan had been offering.[15] Royal garments, ceremonial and private, were loaned or given by the King, Queen Mary and the Dowager Queen Alexandra and there were excavated items such as footwear.

The London Museum was an instant success, with displays of every sort of artefact from archaeological finds to prints and drawings, all designed to tell the story of London's development from prehistory to modern times. This one-subject theme did not disguise the fact that it was now in competition with other, longer-established museums, most notably the British Museum and the Victoria & Albert Museum, over important material that illustrated the capital city's long history. By 1914 the new museum found grand new premises in Lancaster House, courtesy of the philanthropist Sir William Lever, the 1st Lord Leverhulme. Substantial benefactions continued to be made, notably by J G Joicey who sent the museum all sorts of treasures, including three large chests of early costume that he had found in Florence.[16]

The recipe for a successful new museum has not changed a great deal since 1914. It has to provide visitors with an educational attraction that offers entertainment as well as instruction. It must constantly offer new content and presentation. It needs dedicated and imaginative staff, a purposeful leader and committed and well-connected trustees. The London Museum was fortunate in its first Keeper, Guy Laking (1911–19) whose genius for publicity and presentation was underpinned by sound scholarship. He was an acknowledged expert on arms and armour but his interests were eclectic. He was a man who believed that '...dullness in a museum is the deadliest of all sins'.[17] His obvious delight

26. Fashion doll's court dress, probably French, c. 1770
Made from French brocaded silk woven with silver
thread and decorated with silver-gilt braid and silk
flowers, this skirt has a court train at the back. The
proportions – the width of skirt and length of train
and the construction of the boned bodice – are
accurate, which suggests that it is made to scale.
However, the fabric and silver lace are overwhelmingly
fussy and out of proportion because the doll serves
not one but several purposes in promoting fabrics and
trimmings as well as cut and construction.

in the growth of the collection of dress was undisguised; there was no snobbery about the
'low status' of fashion and it is likely that he, with his knowledge of armour, saw dress as
the non-military equivalent and therefore equally worthy of study and display. After his
premature death in 1919 at the young age of 44 there was something of a hiatus, but the
dynamism returned with the appointment of Dr Mortimer Wheeler as Keeper in 1926.
Wheeler was a brilliant young archaeologist but, like Laking, his vision was not a narrow
one. When he gave evidence to the Royal Commission, which in 1927 was enquiring into
National Museums and Galleries, his submission was so effective that it led to
improvements in funding and staffing in order, as the Commission suggested, that it might
'...set a standard for other Museums of its kind'.[18]

During Wheeler's tenure as Keeper, which lasted until 1944, there was a flurry of
purposeful activity. There were temporary exhibitions, improved systems of documentation,
public concerts and increased educational activities for adults and children. Costume
displays were always a crucial element in the story of London and included a figure on
horseback and a criminal in his cell; there was nothing stuffy about how history and the
dress of the past was presented. It is a measure of his success and of the staff who worked
with him that between 1927 and 1937, when attendance figures declined at the National
Gallery, the Tate Gallery and the Victoria & Albert Museum, the London Museum's visitor
figures rose from 276,525 to 364,097.[19] He also encouraged scholarship and from 1927
onwards seven catalogues were published, the fifth of which was Thalassa Cruso's

Collecting dress

Costume, first published in 1933 and reprinted twice in the following 15 years. In a typically idiosyncratic preface to this catalogue Dr Wheeler wrote that, 'Too often in the past has the history of fashion been treated lightly, as a rather inconsequential pageant, an arbitrary and theatrical decoration of history; too rarely has it been regarded as an integral and significant facet of the actual historical structure'.[20]

It was a formidable piece of work and was, deservedly, both influential and popular because it was much more than a catalogue of artefacts. It is arranged in two main sections, the first comprising a series of short essays on the evolution of male and female fashionable dress between 1558 and 1933, illustrated with a range of sources, not just of dress, but caricatures, engravings, and other artefacts from the London Museum's collections. Each sub-section of this historical survey, for instance 'Men's dress from the Restoration to the French Revolution (1660–1790)', is followed by a brief summary illustrated with line drawings taken from dated originals, such as portraits and engravings, all contained on one page to allow the reader to absorb at a glance the changes in appearance and structure of garments. The actual catalogue has a curious hierarchical structure, which offers an insight into the powerful patronage network in which the museum had been cocooned since its foundation in 1911 and strongly emphasized its links with royal and aristocratic patrons. It appeared to have all of the necessary scholarly apparatus for it to sit alongside the other catalogues in that early series, but its chronological narrative of fashion changes would now be considered lacking in depth and analysis, and in some instances the information is flawed. It is, however, more detailed than the actual 'catalogue', of garments which, in many instances, is a very basic list with approximate dates, with imprecise descriptions and no measurements. Both Kohler and Talbot Hughes had given measurements and the former, or his later editor Emma von Sichart, had provided longer descriptions of garments. Kohler and Talbot Hughes had, of course, spent years studying collections and assembling information, but Thalassa Cruso had nothing like their experience before producing, in less than two years after her appointment to the London Museum's staff, the first catalogue in the United Kingdom of a museum collection of dress and accessories. Its reprint within a couple of years and again in 1946 indicated that there was an audience for this type of information on dress in museums. The catalogue, flawed though it was, might well have set a standard to be emulated or surpassed elsewhere. It demonstrated that complete catalogues of dress, as in this instance, or those covering specific periods or topics, could be produced to sit alongside catalogues of ceramics, furniture, paintings and silver.

The London Museum, like many others, was closed for much of World War II but afterwards it had the singular misfortune of losing its home to government hospitality and conference requirements. It took some considerable time before it reopened, at Kensington Palace in a set of apartments much smaller than those at Lancaster House. It used the same formula of mixing costume within chronological displays on London's history and also, for a period, displayed some of its royal costume in the State Apartments of the palace. It, too, acquired staff dedicated to the needs of the large and still growing collection, which in addition to examples of elite fashions also accepted everything from excavated early finds to modern dress, with considerable holdings of royal, ceremonial and theatrical costume.

The Metropolitan Museum of Art In New York was founded in 1886 shortly after the Rijksmuseum opened in its new premises in Amsterdam. The Costume Institute, however, was not originally part of the museum. Its early origins owed much to a small number of like-minded enthusiasts who were interested in the dress of the past. In 1937 the Museum of Costume Art, Costume Institute Inc. was founded under its first President Irene Lewisohn. She and her sister Alice Lewisohn Crowley became interested in costume through their close involvement with experimental theatre in New York and were keen that it should be collected and available for study. Gradually they acquired a collection of European, Middle Eastern and Oriental costume at a time when, as Polaire Weissman wrote, '...there was still no museum farsighted enough to acknowledge the fellowship of costume with other branches of art. At least none was willing as yet to establish its own department of costume. True, there were some museums that had collections of costumes, but such collections were mere stepchildren to the departments of textiles, often poorly accessible to visitors and inadequately equipped for study and service'.[21]

The embryonic Museum of Costume Art moved three times in less than ten years, holding well-received exhibitions and adding to its collections, until it entered the orbit of the Metropolitan Museum in the latter's Diamond Jubilee year in 1946 and a merger was arranged. The press hailed it as a new 'Mecca for the country's style leaders', but its quasi-independence meant that it still needed money and, in 1948, an annual fund-raising event 'The Party of the Year' was introduced.[22] By 1959 the Costume Institute was fully absorbed into the Metropolitan Museum and by 1967 its reputation in terms of its exhibitions and scope of its collections made it 'the most comprehensive in the world' according to Weissman, its first Executive Director.[23] By that time it had accrued enough funds and supporters to undertake a major rebuilding programme and, somewhat later than its European counterparts, also acquired its first professional curator.

Paris has two major costume museums, the longest established being the Musée du Costume de la Ville de Paris (the other is attached to the Louvre). The Musée du Costume opened in 1956 as a branch of the Carnavalet Museum, which had so impressed the founders of the London Museum with its history of the city. The Carnavalet had acquired a collection decades earlier as the result of a donation from the Société de l'Histoire du Costume. This Society had been formed in 1907 by a group of enthusiasts led by artist and dress historian Maurice Leloir, and its members included the French couturier Jean Doucet. The Society wanted to create a museum, an idea that seemed feasible after World War I. An effusive article in *Vogue* in 1920 dismissed other European museums as 'dull tombs' and proposed that what Paris needed was '...a collection both varied and attractive, composed of authentic pieces complete in all details, a collection historically correct and sumptuous, which would not only appeal to the eye, but might serve as an authoritative example of other modes, and thus satisfy both one's curiosity and one's interest in old costumes'.[24] Leloir was the Director of the new Museum of Costume and was robust in defending the Society as a 'public utility' necessary for combating false ideas about the dress of the past: 'True modes are quite as picturesque and infinitely more interesting.

Here in the Museum, costumers, archaeologists, artists, and the interested public shall see the truth at last'.[25] The collection was eclectic in composition, ranging from elite dress to peasant costumes, and included examples from a number of European countries. Its accommodation was temporary, as it waited upon the City of Paris to find a suitable home, though the premises had a tenuous link with one of the most influential of early 20th-century dress, textile and theatre designers. The museum was in the former home of the Spanish painter Raymond de Madrazo, the uncle of Fortuny. The presentation seems to have owed more than a little to Madame Tussaud's approach to historical characters: 'Wax models full of dignity appear almost lifelike, arranged in the ancient costumes so admirably preserved'.[26] The Society's relationship with the City of Paris and the Carnavalet Museum continued, but a permanent and separate museum for costume did not open until 1956. The building in which the new museum was housed and in which it presented annual exhibitions had to be closed in 1971 while more suitable premises were found.

Collectors and their museums: three English examples

All of the major museum collections outlined in the last section benefited from the collecting zeal of many individuals and groups, often with close links to artists and the theatre and/or influential and wealthy patrons. Once such collections were absorbed into larger organizations they had to be well supported in order to fund staff, publication and space for display. The public might like displays of costume but they were not necessarily equally popular within museums. How such private collections, all assembled differently, found their way into museums is instructive. This section considers just three examples, but many more deserve further study in order to identify the taste and ideas of previous generations and to explore whether the ideas of these collectors were in step with the attitudes of their contemporaries. The growth in collecting and the enthusiasm to rescue the dress of the past from oblivion also carried within it a naive assumption that public finance would continue to be available to support such initiatives. It was not dissimilar to rescue archaeology in that stockpiling crucial evidence was perceived to be the first step on the route to widespread acceptance of the need to retain such material for future generations of scholars. The heyday of collecting costume was somewhat earlier. It occurred in the period after World War I, when antique dealers and specialist markets were flooded with all sorts of artefacts from the contents of large houses that were dispersed due to social changes and tougher economic conditions. Obviously some of this material found its way into national and regional museums, often as donations because high market prices and the involvement of auction houses were not yet a factor in the disposal of such items. That this was the ideal time to collect is demonstrated in the case of three very different individuals whose collections eventually found their way in to museums.

The Cunningtons, Dr C Willett (1879–1961) and his wife Phillis (1887–1974), began collecting dress almost by accident. In 1930 he spotted 'a gorgeous-looking old silk dress for sale' in a small Hampstead antique shop. He bought it thinking it might provide fabric for an evening cloak for his wife but decided first to take it to the Victoria & Albert Museum in London for identification. He discovered that it might date from the 1870s but this thin information was not enough to satisfy him and he decided that '...we should have

27. (left) Woman's day dress c. 1879–81 (front and side views); photographs by John Chase
Created from wool crepe and silk satin, the dress is both machine- and hand-sewn. The relatively simple fitted line of the dress is turned into a demonstration of the dressmaker's skill by the use of draping, pleating, ruching and gathering of the two fabrics. By this date it was usual for much of the basic construction to be machine-sewn with some hand finishing. This dress has no label, but could have been bought readymade or made to order, depending upon the circumstances of the purchaser. This is exactly the sort of garment that the Cunningtons thought worth saving in the 1930s when such dresses were appearing in markets and in antique shops.

28. (right) Page from an album of fashion plates, late 19th century; photograph by John Chase
This page spread has a mixture of plates from Le Beau Monde and La Belle Assemblée of 1806. It is the first in a series of four volumes that contain plates from 19th-century magazines. Some information accompanies the plates but this is not dissimilar to an archaeological find without a context: they are attractive but only useful if the original magazines are consulted to add descriptive and contextual information. It was usual to break magazines up and use the plates as inexpensive pictures, not exactly art, but pleasing decorations. Many collectors of dress, including the Cunningtons and Doris Langley Moore, acquired fashion plates and magazines.

to solve our problem-piece by our efforts, and this meant collecting fashion journals of the 19th century and searching in them for more precise evidence'.[27] As the evidence and his costume collection grew in size so did Cunnington's interest in and knowledge of the subject. One important result was *English Women's Clothing in the Nineteenth Century*, published in 1937, a book that Anne Buck described as '...a landmark in the study of costume in this country'.[28] So, in addition to avid collecting, Cunnington had evolved into a dress historian, in effect a more rigorous version of Talbot Hughes whose work was discussed in chapter 1. Cunnington sought out comparative examples in other UK collections while researching his book, and he visited 19 museums. In the short section of the book devoted to museums he is scathing about the Victoria & Albert Museum and Bethnal Green Museum: 'In both these "national" museums the illumination is deplorable (a fault with most of our museums); it is astonishing that no catalogue is obtainable'.[29] He is non-judgmental about the London Museum where 'About 100 dresses of the nineteenth century are displayed ... A catalogue is available'. He saves his warmest comments for the Manchester collection, which was displayed at Platt Hall: 'An excellent collection, admirably displayed, of some 90 dresses ... This collection is rapidly increasing and now rivals any in the country'.[30] His overall view of museum provision is critical and he argued fiercely for an approach beyond that of 'a mere mausoleum for old clothes', believing that social and technical change and material from all social classes and occupations should inform displays. His belief was that, 'The guiding principle should be to collect those specimens which will interest posterity and faithfully portray the past'. His solution was '...a national museum dedicated solely to Costumes and adequately supplied with funds; but it seems that only nations poorer than England can afford that luxury'.[31]

Eventually, after attempts to garner support for this plan in government circles, the clothing industries and among the public, his collection found its home at Platt Hall in Manchester, one of the few places he had found admirable in the 1930s. The complex nature of the negotiations and the piecemeal payment of the £7000 Cunnington was asking for his collection is recounted in an article by Anthea Jarvis in *Costume 33* in 1999.[32] The collection was far from representative when it was first displayed to the public in 1947. It contained practically no menswear and only a few 18th-century examples, and the details of provenance were slight if not wholly missing, as Cunnington confessed: 'I was never particularly interested in the personal aspect & found that family histories about specimens were so unreliable as to be worthless'.[33] This posed problems if the collection was to provide both 'a centre for the study of the art and history of costume' and to be viewed as a contribution to social history.[34] Inevitably the collection had to expand, and by the time that Jane Tozer was writing a critique of the Cunnington approach in 1986 the original 3500 items of costume and accessories accounted for about one sixth of the 1986 total. This is a phenomenal growth in 40 years but was prompted by the wish '...to collect men's, women's and children's costume of the eighteenth century and earlier if possible; to build up a collection of men's clothes; to fill gaps in the existing series and to collect types of dress not already represented; and to keep the collection up to date'.[35]

The Gallery was fortunate in that the Cunningtons continued to be prolific authors, promoting knowledge of the subject and the importance of the Manchester collection. The other stroke of good fortune was that the first Keeper, Anne Buck, was a dedicated professional and, arguably, one of the most influential costume curators to work within the museum sector, not just in the United Kingdom but internationally. Manchester steadily built a national and international reputation for excellence, setting standards in the care, display and publication of its collections.

A somewhat younger contemporary of the Cunningtons was Doris Langley Moore (1902–1989). If the Cunningtons' approach to collecting was sturdily methodical (the medical specimen school of collecting), Mrs Langley Moore's seems to have been, from the outset, somewhat more mercurial. She was an able self-publicist and moved easily in the worlds of fashion, literature and theatre. A glimpse of this can be seen in a lavishly illustrated profile of the collector and her collection published in *Picture Post* in 1951, entitled 'Out of London's Fashion Museum'. One of the captions to an illustration sums up her inimitable approach: 'The Founder of the Museum – Mrs Langley Moore has been collecting costumes for twenty five years, there she is, cataloguing new items, including a Dior dress, given by Madame Massigli, wife of the French ambassador'.[36] This was a new way of collecting: demonstrating an interest in contemporary fashion with a shrewd acknowledgment of the chic circle of friends and acquaintances from whom such donations were acquired.

Mrs Langley Moore, like the Cunningtons, evolved into a published dress historian, not just a collector. Her three books about dress, *The Woman in Fashion* (1949), *The Child in Fashion* (1953) and *Fashion Through Fashion Plates 1771–1970* (1971) give valuable insights into her approach. The use of the word fashion, rather than costume or dress, places her firmly within a new sphere, but she was shrewd enough to use the other terms depending upon the audience for whom she was writing or to whom she was speaking. It seems to have been fashion plates that first interested her. According to her own recollections, she was looking for 'a few pictures to enliven some of the empty walls' of her new house in 1926 when she 'bought ancient fashion plates' and, having a 'collector's blood in my veins, I gradually began to buy fashion plates even when I did not intend to hang them'.[37] The transition to collecting dress came at Christmas 1928, 'when my hostess in a Wensleydale country house produced some old dresses' for charades and then allowed Mrs Langley Moore to keep one that fitted her. A short while later she saw another dress in an antique shop in Harrogate and bought it, thinking that she might 'cut it up and remake it for myself' but paused as her scissors 'were actually hovering over the rich damask'.[38] This is uncannily close to the story of the Cunningtons in 1930 and one wonders if the muse of collecting was working overtime in those couple of years or whether a good story heard elsewhere is adapted to suit other circumstances?

The collection grew and, having moved to London, Mrs Langley Moore began to search for a permanent home for it. By the early 1950s a 'non-profit-making company' called The Fashion Research Centre and Museum of Costume Ltd, which was based at a house in Great Cumberland Place, London, acquired an Arts Council grant.[39] A prospectus was written and sent to possible sponsors. This detailed document described the proposed museum and the many strengths of the collection. A couple of sections from the prospectus indicate Mrs Langley Moore's ambitious intentions:

'Apart from the Cunnington Collection in Manchester, no museum specifically devoted to dress exists in England and very few in the world.

The need for a compact organization offering faculties for the study of costume cannot be met by our great museums, excellent as they are, for these have as yet amassed very little material relating to the recent past, and are seldom able to display the fashions of the present. Moreover, in the large public museums, it is not possible to examine the interior structure and the texture of garments.'

Later, the prospectus adds:

'A museum where feminine clothing and adornments, including jewellery, could be seen in great variety, and where information on costume subjects might be rapidly and easily obtained in pleasant surroundings, would be, it is believed, a show-place of the greatest interest to visitors from abroad, and a means of encouraging design and craftsmanship at home.'[40]

This consummate piece of promotion suggested a Nirvana for general visitors, design students and tourists who could not be served by the Victoria & Albert Museum, the London Museum and Platt Hall. However its emphasis is unchanged: 'feminine clothing and adornments' are its strength. The only difference in Mrs Langley Moore's approach is that she is concerned not just with the past but also with 'the fashions of the present'. In 1970 she told The Costume Society conference that, '...we [the Museum of Costume] are particularly proud of our very fine representation of haute couture of the last fifty years. An outfit for each current year is selected by an eminent fashion expert and proves to be a pleasantly controversial talking point.'[41]

Unlike the Cunningtons, Mrs Langley Moore did not easily find a permanent home for her collection. It opened at Eridge Castle in Kent in 1955 and sometime later moved briefly to the Brighton Pavilion and the Octagon Chapel in Bath. It was suggested that once the Assembly Rooms at Bath were renovated after severe wartime damage the collection could be displayed there. After various negotiations Mrs Langley Moore gave her collection to the City of Bath and the Museum of Costume opened in the Assembly Rooms in 1963. It was a considerable success, due in no small part to the lively presentation, or what Mrs Langley Moore called 'showmanship in costume display'.[42]

The last in this small group of case studies chosen to highlight the hybrid manner in which private collections of costume became an accepted part of museum provision in the United Kingdom, is Chertsey Museum in north-west Surrey. It is a minnow compared to the whales in London, Manchester, Bath and internationally, but it is included because, yet again, its genesis lay in the collection of an individual. Olive Matthews (1887–1979) was an only child brought up in London by a strict father, who was a successful businessman, and his sister's family (her mother had died when she was two). Her early interest in costume seems, in part, to have been prompted by the survival of a few interesting family pieces. The most notable of these is a white linen handkerchief printed in indigo with English playwrights and actors

29. The collector as model, photograph, 1948–9
Here, Mrs Doris Langley Moore is wearing an evening
dress of 1903. Her book The Woman in Fashion,
published in 1949, was one of the methods she used
to promote her collection of costume. The idea of
people wearing clothes from the past in books and
catalogues was prevalent until the 1980s. The two
obvious problems – that this can damage the
garment and that few modern models have the
physique or can find the appropriate underclothes
and corsetry or wish to adopt the hairstyles that suit
the garments – was ignored. It was, however,
preferable to amateur and inaccurate line drawings.

30. Olive Matthews, Chertsey Museum, April 1972
The collector is photographed with one of her
favourite purchases, a brocaded silk dress of the
1740s. She did not write about her collection but was
proud when it was given, in its entirety, into the
curatorial care of a museum, and she was generous
in safeguarding its future well being.

within rococo ribbon borders; embroidered on it is 'Susanna Pearce July the 9 1774'. Susanna Pearce was her ancestress and the 18th century was of continuing fascination to Olive Matthews. She wanted to collect 18th-century furniture but, aware that her father would disapprove, she decided upon artefacts that could easily be hidden in cupboards and boxes: dress and accessories. She began collecting slowly but, in a collecting life that spanned over 40 years, she became familiar with the bargains to be found on market stalls and occasionally from antique dealers. Her main area of interest was the period from c. 1740 to c. 1840, although she did acquire a few earlier and later pieces.

When she moved to Virginia Water in the 1940s her collection accompanied her and was stored in boxes in her house and garage. She had established a rapport with staff at the Victoria & Albert Museum but, when considering what might happen to her collection in the long term, she knew that they would not accept it in its entirety. She lacked the dynamism and ebullience of the Cunningtons and Doris Langley Moore and the existence of her collection was little-known. Fortunately she became friendly with another local collector, Sydney Oliver, and he both understood the importance of her collection and had the local contacts and strong personality to ensure that it remained intact and could form a significant addition to a small local museum. A few miles away from Virginia Water, Chertsey Urban District Council had opened a museum to display a mixture of donations:

ceramics, Greek pottery and local history material. The premises were cramped and inadequate, but re-housed and with the addition of Olive Matthews's collection it would become an interesting local museum. In 1969 the Olive Matthews Collection became a trust and an arrangement was made with Chertsey Urban District Council with regard to funding and responsibilities for the enlarged collections. The trust bought a late Regency house in Chertsey and the two collections came together in a new museum, which opened to the public in 1972. Much of the Olive Matthews Collection – apart from dress and textiles there are accessories, including jewellery, some china, paintings, needlework tools, toys and furniture – was transferred to the museum during her lifetime and the residue after her death in 1979.

There are many differences between Olive Matthews, the Cunningtons and Mrs Langley Moore but a crucial one, for the long-term security of the collection, was that Matthews neither sold nor gave hers to a local authority. Instead she created a trust which continues to administer it along the lines described in the original Deed of Settlement of 1969. The trust owns the collection and is able to negotiate with the local authority (now Runnymede Borough Council) knowing that it has the funds to maintain and enhance the collection. However, apart from this fundamental difference there are others that offer insights into the collecting process. Olive Matthews, unlike the Cunningtons and Doris Langley Moore, was even-handed in her collecting of male and female garments. One of her favourite purchases was a man's suit (coat, waistcoat and breeches) of c. 1780. It is a splendid example of formal dress, tailored from bronze and yellow silk with complex embroidery in silk and metal threads, beads, sequins and seed pearls. Her taste ran to such decorative pieces, to the embroidered, beaded, printed, painted. She bought complete, part and altered pieces of female dress but assembled a fine small collection of menswear. Although she never wrote about her collection and was refreshingly modest about her excellent eye and ability to find good examples, her guiding principle seems to have been that, 'Styles I have known and worn I don't care about. They are not antiques to me'.[43] It is interesting that she thought of her collection as 'antiques', preferring the excellence of past craftsmanship to more modern achievements. In that regard she differed from the Cunningtons, who were rescuing unregarded female clothing of the 19th century, and from Doris Langley Moore, who believed contemporary female fashion was as significant as her earlier items. Private collecting will, inevitably, reflect the interests and tastes of its collectors, but within recent work on dress/fashion such collections are rarely considered. Their existence is accepted, but the reasons for assembling them and the information they can yield about changing views on the dress of the past and present is rarely investigated.

4 The use of collections 1970 to the present

'This is a plea that the real thing finds a place within the research and teaching of all involved in costume history'. N Tarrant in *Costume*[1]

In the examples given in the previous chapter the intention was to demonstrate that having arrived quite late, as a serious area of collecting, dress became an undisputed feature of museum provision between 1950 and 1970. In the post-World War II period, in particular from the 1960s onwards, there was a growth in general museum provision and an acceptance that collections of dress offered some tangible understanding of an occupied past. Costumed figures helped to create the idea of how owners of ceramics, furniture, paintings and metalwork – the strengths of many collections – might have looked. Admittedly some of these figures were unrealistic, headless or with a shape that seemed at odds with their garments, but visitors to museums throughout the United Kingdom, in Europe and North America were offered an extra dimension, something approximating people. That most of these 'people' were from elite groups in society was not spelt out, but neither was the status of owners of ceramics, furniture and other artefacts. Relativities in social status and the need to redress the balance towards consideration of the majority of the population was a feature of later collecting and display.

31. (bottom left) Waistcoat fronts c. 1770–75; photograph by John Chase
The two panels are of silk satin decorated with embroidery in coloured silks, metal thread, chenille, paste stones and mirror glass sequins. One embroidered pocket is tacked onto the left front to show the finished effect, and a row of 12 outlined button shapes are on the right front vertical edge. Enough of these waistcoat fronts survive in museum collections to indicate that a system existed for allowing the customer to decide between a number of different embroidered patterns before the waistcoat was made up. The amount of unembroidered fabric would enable the finished waistcoat to fit most clients if they were neither very tall nor very short in stature. This type of pale ground with an overall pattern, with detailed effects concentrated on the front, buttons and pocket flaps is found from the 1760s onwards, more especially for evening wear as the jewelled and sequinned details would catch the light in candlelit rooms as the wearer moved.

32. (opposite page, bottom right). Detail from a man's waistcoat c. 1775–80
This silk waistcoat is decorated with multi-coloured silk and metal threads and sequin embroidery. The ground embroidery is simpler than in the previous example and all the complex embroidery effects are concentrated along the edges and both on and below the pocket flaps. The embroidery motifs, using various combinations of flowers, grasses and leaves, is typical of these waistcoats and, long after they ceased to be fashionable evening dress they survived as formal court wear.

33. Evening dress, English, c, 1900
This comprises a bodice and skirt of duchesse satin with asymmetrical embroidery of silks, metal threads and glass beads, with the label of Madame Clapham, Kingston Square, Hull. The consuming interest in the great couturiers of the post-Worth period overlooks the importance of the hundreds of dressmaking businesses throughout Europe and America that existed well into the 20th century. This remarkable Yorkshire-based dressmaker's career began with a dressmaking apprenticeship at Marshall and Snelgrove in Scarborough. She owned her own establishment from 1887 up until her death in 1952 and her successful business has been painstakingly traced and recorded by a curator at Kingston-upon-Hull Museum. Her clientele included fashionable society figures in London and Yorkshire and she provided clothes for Queen Maud of Norway, daughter of Edward VII. There were no business records, just surviving garments and interviews with former employees and patrons. This is the best form of museum detective work, deriving clues from material within a collection and building out from them to create a record of a business in which women excelled.

As collections grew and developed in quantity and the time-span they covered, they were cared for more systematically. Anne Buck and colleagues of her generation met and discussed how best to look after and present these newly reputable collections. They exchanged views on documentation or the record of each artefact, how it might be best stored, conserved, handled and presented to the public. More specialist costume curators were appointed in museums of varying size and location. Cheaper and faster travel allowed curators from all countries with collections to discuss their work face to face and agree upon international standards under the umbrella organization of the International Council of Museums (ICOM). It also became easier to attend conferences, study days and symposia arranged by the many specialist groups and societies that had begun to concern themselves with dress and textiles. Such groups ranged from broadly based membership – the Costume Society in the United Kingdom, the Costume Society of America, and similar societies in Europe – and professional bodies like the Group for Costume & Textiles Staff in Museums, formed in 1975 for full- or part-time curators of dress collections. The popularity of collections with a broad cross-section of museum visitors, from children undertaking school projects to dedicated researchers, meant that displays were complemented by a variety of publications. These included postcards, slides, short catalogues of a period or type of garment, leaflets, photographs and other items such as reproduction fashion plates, cut-out dolls and lace sample sheets.

This was an optimistic period of expansion, with galleries and branch museums of local or regional interest being opened, and country houses also noting the popularity of dress and finding family garments to display or, in some instances acquiring and building collections, such as the one at Castle Howard in Yorkshire, which opened in 1965.[2] No-one undertook feasibility studies to calculate the long-term expenses involved in these initiatives; the prevailing optimism did not allow for uncertainty about the future. Even then staffing and facilities were often minimal, as it was assumed that improvement would be incremental. The one fact that invariably surprises researchers and museum professionals without knowledge of dress collections is the huge amount of hands-on labour that curating dress to tolerable standards requires. Preparing detailed inventories, regularly checking stored collections for damp, pests and other hazards, getting out and then returning material required by researchers and students and the preparation of garments for display takes much longer for a curator of dress than for their colleagues who curate ceramics, paintings or furniture. Volunteers and friends' organizations are invaluable allies in the housekeeping aspects of this work, but volunteers cannot be expected to take responsibility for research, exhibitions and education, and all of these have to be fitted around the edges of caring for collections. This chapter will consider how the shifting perceptions of the position of dress within a museum environment have created problems in the late 20th and early 21st centuries.

Permanent and temporary: galleries and exhibitions

Looking again briefly at the museums and collections used as examples in the previous chapter, it is apparent that there were differing attitudes to the presentation of collections to the public. Some depended upon permanent displays with occasional temporary exhibitions, others concentrated on short-lived exhibitions accompanied by catalogues or books, yet others found themselves without any display facilities for long periods of time. Although temporary exhibitions had been a feature in some museums from the outset, it was from the 1970s onwards that all museums began to realize that static, unchanging displays could not satisfy the increasingly sophisticated tastes of populations who travelled more, had many more choices of how and where to spend their free time and money, and were used to the movement, sound and presentation found in films and on television. Inanimate and didactic museum displays seemed frozen in a previous, less demanding age. The Victoria & Albert Museum in London presented Fashion: An Anthology by Cecil Beaton in 1971, and at the end of the exhibition acquired over 200 well-documented garments and accessories, the work of many of the great couturiers. A couple of years later the London Museum celebrated Mary Quant's London, an early retrospective display of a contemporary British designer, while the work of Jean Muir was exhibited between 1980 and 1981 in venues in Leeds, Birmingham, Belfast and Bath. This was not dissimilar to the successful approach adopted in Paris and New York.

Although the Musée du Costume in Paris had closed in 1971 this did not deter the curator Madeleine Delpierre from producing a book to celebrate the museum's 20th anniversary in 1976. Its title *Vingt Ans Après ... Principaux Enrichissements 1956–1976* recorded how the museum had acquired gifts, not just from the Société de l'Histoire du Costume, but also from individuals and major couturiers. The collection encompassed men's, women's and children's clothing, accessories and underclothes, and also civic and ceremonial garments and robes. When the museum finally reopened at its new home in the Palais Galliera in 1977 it chose to celebrate the glories of recent French fashion in an exhibition entitled Paris 1945–1975: Élégance et Création. The catalogue demonstrated the generosity of great designers, with pieces from Balenciaga, Balmain, Cardin, Chanel, Dior, Lanvin and many more. The new location was accompanied by a new name, Musée de la Mode et du Costume, which emphasized the museum's role in collecting and displaying fashion as well as historic costume. While never as populist as the Costume Institute in New York, it combined serious scholarship (its catalogues are never merely picture books with captions of wonderful clothes) with an understanding of the need to vary exhibitions on historic themes with ones that celebrated recent fashion in a city that is one of the major world centres of fashion.

In New York there was a four-year rebuilding and consolidation phase at the Costume Institute, during which its first full-time curator, Stella Blum, was appointed. It reopened in the autumn of 1971 with an exhibition called The Fashion Plate, which considered the similarities and discrepancies between the idealized image and the reality of surviving dress. By 1972 Diana Vreeland had been appointed as Special Consultant for Exhibitions and, in Stella Blum's generous words, 'Her initial exhibition, The World of Balenciaga, introduced a brand new approach to costume exhibitions, in a spectacular setting a fashion designer for the first time was given the focus reserved in museums for great artists'.[3]

Diana Vreeland had been Fashion Editor at *Harper's Bazaar* and Editor-in-Chief at *Vogue* before she was summoned to the Costume Institute. She was both ageless though old, and charming but egocentric, and had a contacts book like no other. As a discreetly critical obituary written by someone who had been involved tangentially with her work noted: 'There were times when she had difficulty understanding curatorial codes and ethics, but she knew the effect she wanted her exhibitions to have and the exhibitions were always enormous social occasions'[4]. Vreeland's success and monstrous ego overshadowed her talented but self-effacing colleague Stella Blum, the professional curator of the Costume Institute. Riding roughshod over curatorship and colleagues, Diana Vreeland reinvented costume exhibitions as glossy extravaganzas, fashionable social occasions, and introduced the concept of the hagiography of living designers. After her death in 1989 there were no more Special Consultants at the Costume Institute, but she had set a pattern that is still being followed: glamour, erratic scholarship and maximum celebrity appeal. It is a heady mix – fashion as spectacular theatre – and its impact has permeated well beyond America.

The Rijksmuseum in Amsterdam, not dissimilar to the Victoria & Albert Museum and the Metropolitan Museum in its great collections and lure to visitors, had chronological displays in period room-settings until these were withdrawn in the mid-1980s. Occasional small displays appeared elsewhere in the museum until the creation of a new Costume and Textiles Gallery in 1996, which opened with the temporary exhibition Nothing But The Best, a selection of some of the finest female examples from the mid-18th century up to 1979. In other museums in the post-1970 period permanent displays, dedicated galleries or branch museums opened with differing approaches. Dress was displayed as social history or as a decorative art, it was included in permanent galleries or temporary exhibitions, which might be thematic or offer a narrative of the changes in fashion. In Manchester there was a combination of both chronological displays and temporary exhibitions and a similar pattern was followed at Bath after renovations to the building in the late 1970s. Also in Bath, Doris Langley Moore finally achieved a Fashion Research Centre in a Georgian house a short walk from the Museum of Costume. The London Museum, reconstituted as the Museum of London in 1975, had dress and textiles within the chronological history of the capital and presented small temporary exhibitions on a number of themes, usually drawing upon the strengths of its own collections. In Chertsey from the outset there was always one room devoted to displays of dress and these changed every few years.

Unfortunately the care of dress and textiles collections is expensive and as advances were made in the correct environment and storage facilities, it became apparent that these collections took up a great deal of space and were increasingly labour-intensive if regular new displays were to be presented and maintained to accepted standards. The cost of running museums attracted attention and began to be scrutinized rigorously by funding bodies that, generally speaking, are often badly informed, not interested in cultural issues or, occasionally, vociferously opposed to what is perceived as elitist culture. There was also the introduction of competitive factors: seeking sponsors, measuring visitor numbers and finding new ideas for display among a diminishing pool of all of these. Imperceptibly at

34. Display of dress, Chertsey Museum, 2004;
photograph by John Chase
Modern curators prefer themes to chronological
surveys of dress/fashion and, if they are familiar with
their collections, want to find appropriate ideas from
within the resources at their disposal rather than rely
on loans from other museums. The idea that displays
of clothing divorced from the human figure are
merely informative about stylistic change and
technical innovation tends to overlook the
imaginative role of the curator. One of the principal
roles of a skilful curator is to offer methods of
interpretation that reflect the interests of their users.
Consultations with all users, whether educational,
informed or curious, will form part of the process of
deciding what should be displayed and, within
conservation requirements, how it should be
displayed. Collections of dress and textiles are central
to the understanding of how individuals and groups
in modern society consider the past.

35. Accessories, Chertsey Museum, 2004; photograph
by John Chase
The costume display can deconstruct elements of
dress and accessories and, in many respects, adopts a
similar approach to that found in a large department
store. Hats, bags, shoes and scarves are usually found
in separate parts of the store, and groups of
accessories displayed in museums are often separate
from the garments they once complemented. There
are advantages and disadvantages to this type of
display: it assists the student interested in the
evolution of hats or fans and changes in technique
or decoration but removes them from immediate
proximity to suits or dresses. However, the past
cannot be accurately reconstructed; what we see is
mediated by the expertise and knowledge of the
curator and the constraints of presentation informed
by the best form of care for the artefacts.

first, a gulf was opening up between the display of contemporary fashion and the cultivation of those rich and famous enough to afford such clothes, and the display of dress from earlier periods, sometimes associated with dimly remembered figures from history but often anonymous and therefore perceived as less relevant.

As far back as 1994 Naomi Tarrant, the then Curator of Costume at the National Museums of Scotland wrote, 'In museums costume is at present being marginalised. Art-based departments view the topic with distrust. For social history departments, costume is a very small part of an overall picture and the elite nature of many of the surviving objects is regarded with suspicion by some curators'.[5] This quotation is taken from a longer discussion of how and why these problems might have arisen, and her book *The Development of Costume* is essential reading for anyone interested in an intelligent and informed discussion of object-based dress studies. She revisited this topic in an article published in 1999, in which she made the point that, 'After an amazing period of growth, costume collections in museums have run into problems, with several directors questioning their usefulness. This questioning of the place of clothes in a museum is a flawed one. No one questions the collecting of porcelain, nor do they complain that the pottery of ordinary people is not found in museums, a frequent complaint levelled at costume collections'.[6] Her article argued powerfully for the importance of museum dress collections in their totality not just ones that deal with modern designers. In her final words she pinpoints one of the difficulties: '...more and more courses [are] being offered in universities and other institutions which relate to dress and clothing in some way, may I, as a curator of original garments, therefore make a plea that the real thing finds a place within the research and teaching of all involved in costume history?'[7]

This imbalance between the upturn in cross-disciplinary studies of dress, many of which deal mainly with the post-1850 period (the supposed beginning of 'modern' fashion), and the downturn in the status of museum collections that contain dress from the late 17th century onwards is potentially detrimental to any balanced understanding of the subject. Curators fighting for collections are not well placed to devise innovative methods of making the dress of the pre-1850 period relevant to a wider public and not just the dedicated researcher.

Lost opportunities or new directions?

So, five years on, is it any better for costume curators and their collections than when Naomi Tarrant was writing in 1999? In some ways it is much worse, although there are signs of hope. The bad news for all students of the subject is that some collections of costume are without a dedicated curator, as when they leave or retire their posts are being frozen or the funds are diverted elsewhere. Specialist museums of costume and textiles are being threatened with limited opening hours or are being moved and merged with other types of collection, and even the most important collections are absorbed into super-departments of decorative arts, furniture or social history. Few curators of dress and textiles ever become directors of museums, so that the case for this type of collection is usually under-represented in discussions at the highest levels. Also, and this is probably more pertinent to decision making in cash-strapped museum services, there is a frantic pursuit of the latest trends in visitor interests, what one director memorably called the 'death, sex, and jewels' approach to exhibition planning. Nowadays, death, sex and jewels have been overtaken by rare and expensive art, which is wonderfully televisual, unknown but fascinating early societies and anything that has a celebrity tie-in, Armani, Gucci, Prada, and Versace springing irresistibly to mind. It is fascinating that the great Italian artists of the Renaissance vie for curatorial and public attention with the famous Italian fashion houses of today. It cannot be irrelevant that most of the clothes and accessories designed and worn now can be displayed easily on contemporary shop display figures, with no conservation, no tedious individualized display figures, sometimes not even environmental controls or glass cases to spoil the sense of immediacy. Naturally, at a time when budgets for new acquisitions to collections are frozen or falling in real terms, it makes good sense for museums to build strong links with contemporary designers. There is the likelihood of gifts to museum collections which will be important for future generations of curators, students, and visitors, but is this too much of a one-way street, and is it unbalancing collections in favour of a narrow type of collecting? Sophisticated and powerful fashion houses, often part of one of the huge luxury goods conglomerates, gain considerable credibility as well as a new type of publicity when they are associated with a museum. It adds a dimension of academic kudos to already over-inflated egos. In a multicultural society surely a local, regional or national museum should take account of all styles of dress, not just those that reflect the seasonal output of European and North American fashion designers?

There has been discussion for some years that the museum profession cannot provide the right type of leadership, and experimental courses have or are being set up to strengthen the skills needed in the equivalent of a Chief Executive in charge of considerable and complex resources. There is also uncertainty about curatorship: it is increasingly rare within a contract culture for entrants to the profession to build incremental skills and 'learn' their collections thoroughly, and research time is often limited. In every museum there is a juggling of time and resources to meet public expectations, to raise funds and to compete for audiences. The last explains the reliance on temporary exhibitions and the constant search for the 'money-spinner', which in attracting new visitors might persuade some of them to return for other displays and events. Within this highly pressurized environment planning for the future of collections may seem idealistic, but that is happening within museums with acute problems and elsewhere in the museum sector. The Museums Association in Great Britain is undertaking an enquiry to consider three broad questions, broken down into specifics within each category. Firstly, how can museums ensure that their collections will be suited to the needs of users in 2050; secondly, how can museums make more and better use of their collections, and last, would a more strategic and collaborative approach to collecting and the use of collections be beneficial?[8] Obviously this investigation will cover all types of collection but if those three questions were applied solely to costume collections, there are no straightforward answers.

Closures and partnerships

One of the most useful elements in a book like this, which is intended to focus on using sources of information about how to study dress, would be to list where collections can be seen on display or studied by appointment. However, the trends noted earlier – the loss of skilled curators, the closing of galleries or branch museums – has accelerated so fast in the United Kingdom that this is no longer practical. Both nationally funded and local authority museums are under financial pressure and many collections, including costume, have become vulnerable. What is sometimes given as a reason for changes in provision is the location of the museum, the need to create a new type of centre, the prior needs of another collection, the usefulness of websites as a source of information and a lack of public interest. There will be no easy answers and no quick fixes, but visitor demand, measured and recorded, is a crucial factor. Collections need to be studied and published in new ways or they will be forgotten and, in particularly acute circumstances, neglected by default. Looking again at the museums that formed part of the selective history of collecting, can any pattern of innovative new provision be found?

At the Victoria & Albert Museum the dress of the early periods no longer forms part of the Costume Court, although some important examples can be seen in the British Galleries. Temporary exhibitions are held within the Costume Court and leading fashion designers provide an occasional series of fashion shows. A recent innovation is a film, *400 Years of Fashion, anatomy of a collection*, which will obviously be of use to students, researchers and collectors. Perhaps this is a new form of catalogue but will it be possible for other museums to find the resources to follow this example? The Museum of London has the integrated approach of a social history museum and dress is found throughout the galleries and in special exhibitions. The Gallery of English Costume at Manchester is closed to the public except for the last Saturday in each month, but is open to researchers and student groups by appointment. The long-term objective is to move the collections and, in conjunction with Manchester Metropolitan University, create A Centre of Excellence for Fashion and Textiles. This is one element in a strategy to develop Manchester as a Knowledge Capital, intended to give the city a similar status to Antwerp, Lyons and New York as a recognized centre of fashion and textiles design and production.[9] How long this will take and where such a centre will be located is uncertain.

The stand-alone costume museum, a model used in a number of places in the United Kingdom and abroad – in Bath, Leicester, Nottingham, the Hague in the Netherlands, became increasingly neither financially nor culturally viable in the late 20th and early 21st centuries. The Museum of Costume at Bath continues to be popular with the public, but the financial stringencies found throughout the local authority sector in the United Kingdom led to the closure of the Fashion Research Centre in 2003 and the transfer of the material to the Assembly Rooms, and staffing has also diminished in the last few years. Interestingly it is one of the smallest British collections, that of Olive Matthews at Chertsey Museum, which has thrived in recent years. The reason is simple: its unique funding base. The Collection has a sound financial investment portfolio, which enabled the trustees to purchase additional buildings for storage, extend the existing museum, purchase acquisitions, conserve the collection and support certain staff costs. This explains why, in a

36. Evening dress c. 1935
This silk crepe and wool jersey dress with bead embroidery was designed by Norman Hartnell. What type of figure to use for displays of dress is a matter of personal preference, what the budget will provide, and what best suits the particular garment. This photograph offers a clever way of providing information, with the name of the designer disguising the head and concentrating attention on to the dress rather than the display figure.

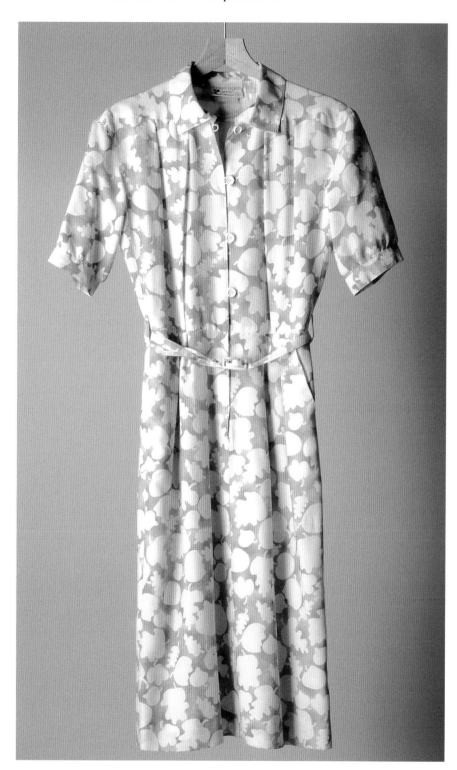

37. Day dress c. 1969; photograph by John Chase
This wool and silk fabric dress with a printed design
of leaves has a label stating, 'Courrèges, Paris made
in France'. This type of simple shirtwaist dress is not
usually associated with the most innovative designer
of the 1960s but its cool colours and simplicity of line
place it within the ready-to-wear collections he
produced from the late 1960s. However without the
label it would be difficult to identify and might not
have found its way into a museum collection.

time when many dress and textiles collections, both public and private, are suffering cutbacks in funding, premises, staff and any form of development, Chertsey Museum is flourishing. Obviously this is not a pattern that can be readily applied elsewhere, but it does emphasize the need for endowment and powerful advocacy to safeguard collections. One-off sponsorship or grants may improve a situation temporarily, but only regular income dedicated to all aspects of work offers real guarantees for the long-term future.

In all of the discussions about the present circumstances, it can be easy to overlook the user of dress collections. The educational impetus that placed information ahead of entertainment in the early years of the formation of such collections has been turned upside down. Conferences, seminars and study days are no replacement for the student who needs to slip regularly into a gallery to draw, make notes and identify what, if anything, the dress of the past can tell us about contemporary fashion. Appointments to view a small selection of pieces not on display are of short duration, although supremely useful when considering construction and technique, but the chronological display was and is one of the best ways of thinking about changes in everything from style to the part that clothing played in determining social roles and attitudes towards fashion. The temporary exhibition, although supremely entertaining, focuses attention on what curators and their colleagues find interesting, and this will give a partial view of the past. In the case of living designers it will, inevitably, reflect their ideas of how they want their work presented. This does nothing to sharpen critical faculties in a fashion student, as they need to know what Armani considers his failures alongside his many successes and who has influenced his work. This has and always will be the insoluble problem both within contemporary collecting and in devising a retrospective of the work of any living artist or craftsman: what will be important in 20, 50 or 100 years time? The curator may be better equipped than the designer to make such a judgment but both are disadvantaged by a lack of objective distance.

Fortunately, there are examples of new ideas for partnerships that will use collections intelligently and, consequently, allow students new forms of information and ways of studying dress. These straddle both the museum and academic sectors, offering comfort to those who had begun to believe that these two areas were, increasingly, mutually exclusive. Such developments have been devised as a result of intellectual application, lateral thinking or sheer expediency combined with a belief in the validity of the subject. An obvious model is FIT – the Fashion Institute of Technology in New York – where students study fashion and textiles, have access to collections and libraries, are taught by skilled curators and lecturers and can see how exhibitions as well as fashion shows are devised. This approach is certainly one that Manchester has absorbed and something allied to it is happening in Leicestershire. Leicestershire, in the Midlands of England, has a long history of fashion industries: knitting, boot and shoe making, female corsetry manufacture and retailing centres. Prior to a local government reorganization in 1997 Leicestershire County Council Museums Service had been responsible for all museum provision, including a Costume Museum in the city of Leicester and Snibston Discovery Park in Coalville. After the reorganization three museum providers emerged: Leicester City Museums Service, Leicestershire County Council Heritage Services and Rutland Museum Service.

The use of collections 1970 to the present

Under the new arrangements Leicester City Museums Service took over responsibility for the Costume Museum, which has since closed, while Leicestershire County Council Heritage Services became responsible for Snibston Discovery Park. The latter was popular with visitors and attracted 100,000 visitors each year. Again, as the result of the changes, a collections-sharing agreement was devised, which allowed both city and county to develop individual strategies for the future. Leicestershire became the leading authority for the display and interpretation of fashionable dress and curates a collection of approximately 20,000 garments dating from 1750 to the present day. A gallery of 1000 square metres, with a designated area for temporary exhibitions, acts as a showcase for the collection, tells the story of the local fashion industries, provides temporary exhibitions and fashion shows, and opportunities to meet well-known designers and fashion journalists. In addition to providing a vibrant service for general visitors, close links have been established with De Montfort University in Leicester, Loughborough University School of Art and Design, and Nottingham Trent University. The Keeper of Cultural Life, a title that encompasses his roles as a curator of fine art, dress and textiles, liaises with all three colleges, sets projects and supervises fashion students, who are introduced to collections that can provide ideas for their work. There is also a close link with the fashion company Next which, from the early 1980s onwards, provided a male and female outfit each season. These enter the collection fully documented as a record of how fashion is interpreted by a major High Street clothing manufacturer.

These local and regional connections between the collection, fashion industries, colleges and local opinion formers were a significant element in the successful bid to the National Heritage Lottery Fund for funding to create a completely new gallery due to open to the public in April 2005. It will be a resource for students and all visitors interested in fashion both historically and in contemporary life. There will be 200 figures arranged in thematic displays that explore topics such as why clothes are worn, the properties of fabrics and their use for garments, how ideas of beauty have changed and the processes of production and retailing. A significant element within this scheme is that there will be a new type of database placed in the gallery. It will provide information about other collections and access to them, details about local courses (25% of students train locally), and what types of jobs are available across the range of the fashion industry. This approach places collections and their use firmly into the fashion industry, a connection which is gradually becoming more widely accepted and will be further enhanced by this database.[10]

Another, more recent example of collaboration between a museum and a college is that formed between the Museum of Costume in Bath and the School of Art and Design at Bath Spa University College. The College created a new course, BA in Fashion Design Skills, and made contact with the Museum of Costume about a partnership. The new course is run from the building that formally housed the Fashion Research Centre and the Keeper of Costume co-teaches the Contextual Studies module on the course. This involves the study and analysis of material from the museum collection and takes place within the study facilities in the main Museum of Costume building at the Assembly Rooms. This purposeful rather than occasional opportunity for students to see, examine, discuss, understand and absorb the styles, colours, techniques and skills that dress collections can offer is obviously not something that can be

quickly applied elsewhere, but it offers another model for collaborations that place collections within fashion rather than as an historical footnote to them.[11]

The last example is different again. A project at the University of Southampton, funded by the Arts & Humanities Research Board (AHRB), began in October 2003 and will end in March 2006. The project is entitled Pockets of History: Production and Consumption of Women's Tie-on Pockets in Britain from c. 1690 to 1914, and is based at the Centre for the History of Textiles and Dress on the Winchester campus of the University. The Centre is justifiably proud of what it calls its '...unique group of textile and textile-related activities and specialists'.[12] This group of individuals and activities include research students and MA programmes in the history of textiles and dress, textile conservation, textile design, European fashion and textile design, textile art, and the Textile Conservation Centre, which has an AHRB Research Centre for Textile Conservation and Textile Studies. Powerful clusters of activity such as these have their own dynamism, producing innovative new programmes of research and public presentation.

38. Girls' dresses, c. 1882–90 (left) and c. 1790–1800 Both dresses have histories of use and re-use. The muslin girl's dress with tambour work embroidery was accompanied by a handwritten note: 'Worked by my Grandmother for her trousseau 1776 afterwards made up for one of her children'. The later dress derives its inspiration from a workman's smock but has been elaborated into a miniature parody of adult styles with the use of coloured silk embroideries, velvet bows and machine lace edging. There are signs that it may have been made in about 1882–4 and altered in c. 1890, although without documentary evidence the reason for this type of alteration can only be surmised; possibly it was altered for a younger sibling.

The project itself will examine the production, consumption, material forms and significance of women's tie-on pockets from the late 17th century to their disappearance in the early 20th century. It will consider both the home-made varieties and those that were commercially manufactured. The evidence that will be used is taken from material culture – the many surviving pockets scattered through British collections – and documentary, literary and visual material. The intention is to give the artefacts and their production and use the broadest of cultural contexts – social class, regional and generational differences of form and use – and to consider certain key questions: 'what were the principal determinants and elements of the tie-on pocket's production and material forms over the period?; how and when was it used?; what does its use reveal about women's lives and roles over time?'[13] As the results are seen as being of interest to differing audiences the research will be presented in a number of formats. There will be a book by an academic publisher, selected papers for conferences and articles and there will be a symposium, exhibition and web site. Pilot material will be shown on the web sites of contributing museums and for smaller museums there will be booklets.

This is a project led by an academic dress historian and a research associate, with museums providing evidence. It is not, strictly speaking, a collaboration of the sort seen in the two earlier examples. It does, though, offer exactly the type of mapping exercise that has so rarely occurred in the United Kingdom. Doctoral students in search of unpublished aspects of material culture have much potential to explore within collections of dress and textiles, and projects such as this may encourage them to do so. It is, of course, not a level playing field. There is no equivalent of an AHRB for museums and therefore partnerships have to be found with university departments who have to act as the lead partner and, understandably, the lead partner may have different ideas on what aspects of collections fit within the research interests of their departments. Persistence and good results may shift the balance as more such partnerships develop. As a colleague wrote to me: 'It is a hard time for costume museums and, as we have all said, one of the ways we can get through this is to form partnerships ... as with many things it is down to the vision and oomph of an individual to make things happen'.[14] The one obvious flaw in this optimistic discussion of new opportunities is that if specialist curators are disappearing faster than they can be replaced or pass on their skills, where will the knowledgeable museum-based partners be found? The only real answer is regular public pressure from students, lecturers, informed visitors and everyone who cares for collections to demand the best. It is also up to users to ask for new types of access and information so that demand can be measured and reported to funding bodies until a case can be made for investment rather than reduction in funding. A book, an article, a display behind glass, a web site can offer some information but informed interpretation by an experienced curator adds immeasurably to understanding the usefulness of collections.

5 Dress in art and dress as art

'I see little justification for continuing to produce works on dress which are only illustrated by works of art; if there are surviving garments, why not show them?' Jane Tozer[1]

'I would certainly not affirm that fashion is *not* art ... But this is something for others to judge'. André Courrèges[2]

The emphasis on studying dress as an adjunct to the history of the fine and decorative arts has a respectable history and heavyweight advocates, as we saw in chapter 1. This is hardly an unusual state of affairs; in many areas of life it makes good sense to be an ally, if sometimes an unwilling one, of the powerful consensus. The natural alliance for dress historians within academic circles seemed to be with art historians and it is unsurprising that the first postgraduate history of dress course in the world was introduced at the Courtauld Institute of Art in 1965. Its founder, Stella Mary Newton, had previously worked at the National Gallery, contributing her expertise to the important series of catalogues compiled there from the 1950s onwards. Many of the early students of the postgraduate course were viewed with suspicion as they began careers in curatorship, lecturing and writing. The small annual intake of students and the lack of serious competition from other universities fostered this idea of a privileged caste destined to interpret dress only within fine art or as an art.

Jane Tozer's remark given at the head of this chapter may or may not have been aimed at the Courtauld approach to dress history. By the mid-1980s those Courtauld-trained students who worked in museums were as interested as Jane Tozer in the diversity of dress studies; dress as material culture or social history was as relevant as dress as an applied or decorative art. The important point about this Courtauld course was that its founder had *not* been trained as an art historian. Stella Newton (1901–2001), doyenne of academic dress historians and both a terrifying and inspirational teacher, had not studied anything in a formal way. She had been a minor actress, a dress designer and a designer of theatrical costume; among her most notable commissions were the costumes for the first production of T S Eliot's *Murder in the Cathedral*. Her husband, Eric Newton, was a distinguished art critic and writer with a particular interest in Venetian art, but who influenced who is uncertain. It was probably a fairly equal match. She could look at paintings with the practical discernment of someone who knew how clothes were made, and how fashions were disseminated and adjusted for the purposes of performance. In truth, all dress in art is a type of performance, the equivalent of deciding, editing, consulting about what is worn for a sitting which, in some medium or other, will be captured for posterity.

There is an obvious problem with the history of dress in all of its manifestations and that is although textiles survive from early periods and cultures of recorded history, actual garments do not provide an uninterrupted flow of evidence across the same long time-span.

Therefore to give the study of dress equal significance to other areas such as architecture, painting, prints, drawings and sculpture, it was inevitable that these other areas would provide much of the source material. The history of surviving dress really only starts in the 17th century, and like all artefacts described as fine or decorative art, is a highly visual subject. However, unlike most of the categories of collection and study that make up those areas, it is fluid rather than static. Garments should be seen in movement on a human body, not frozen on a display figure. This is one of the many difficulties when curating collections of costume and also why some modern writers find costume collections physically and intellectually lifeless. Fortunately, in the period after 1660, when more items of dress survive to enrich our understanding of the history of the subject, there are also many painted, printed, photographed and filmed sources of evidence of people in clothing, caught in movement – too many for easy assimilation. Often a variety of different types of illustrative example will provide evidence about how a garment was worn within the period in which it was made. Without the information contained in art in all of its forms, from drawing to sculpture, it is likely that displays of historic dress would be awkward pastiches of the intentions of their original makers and owners.

The benefits of research that uses both the information inherent in a garment and two-dimensional images are discussed in an article, 'Sleuthing at the Seams' published in 1971.[3] The Costume Institute in New York owned three 18th-century women's dresses that had been altered for later use or for fancy dress but were capable of being reconstructed. The practical knowledge and skills of a conservator, and the ample surviving prints and paintings, offered the mix of evidence required for the painstaking tasks involved. The article uses before and after images of the dresses: a rare English wool mantua of 1690–95; a French striped silk of c. 1760 but altered in c. 1785; an American dress of imported Chinese painted silk, again of 1785 but altered in the 1830s. The French striped silk could not be reconstructed as the dress of c. 1760 but its 1785 lines were recaptured, as were the original construction of both of the others. The 'sleuthing' process described careful examination of the garments to discover original construction, and this was aided by the prints and paintings that could be consulted; a few of these also illustrated the article. This demonstrated a fruitful alliance between the two-dimensional image and the three-dimensional artefact.

The whole discussion of dress in art and dress as art is complicated by the use and misuse of the term 'art'. The dictionary gives numerous definitions but perhaps the most significant is given as: 'Skill applied to the arts of imitation and design, Painting, Architecture, etc.; the cultivation of these in its principles, practice and results', which is described as the usual modern meaning dating from 1668. The dictionary also lists an earlier usage of 1597: 'An occupation in which skill is employed to gratify taste or produce what is beautiful'. However, within academic hierarchies, the arts of painting, architecture etc. have long been considered superior to the more artisan or craft-like skills of ceramics, furniture and metalwork and, of course, dress. Few art historians would consider dress other than an applied or decorative art. The clothed figures that confront them in drawings, paintings, prints and sculpture can still be described with careless inaccuracy or not even mentioned. Baffled art historians, usually with an exhibition catalogue to write, sometimes naively assume that if they speed-read a few books on dress history, they will be able to get by and then misidentify fabrics, use incorrect terms, and so forth. One notable exception to this rule was the late David Piper. His book *The English Face*, originally published in 1957 but reissued in 1978 and again in a revised edition in 1992, provided the type of context about the production of portraiture in England from the 12th century to the Edwardian period that is peerless in its discussion of artists' methods, the conventions of portraiture, concepts of beauty, the role of clothing and cosmetics, and changing views on what constituted a distinctly English appearance. Piper used the work of dress historians with care and discernment, but his example is still unusual even among art historians who curate more portraits than other types of painting. Dress consultants to art galleries are still a rarity despite pioneering work by James Laver, Stella Newton and Aileen Ribeiro.

Dress in art

This is not a book about dress in art and this chapter is intended only to summarize the strengths and some of the well-known problems inherent in this approach. It trains the eye as well as any other method available to the student of dress and by using comparative material from different media – drawings, paintings, prints and sculpture – it allows the student to reach a certain degree of discernment about its usefulness. The study of this material offers the opportunity to discover how and why certain artists, often not the finest, are more reliable sources for historians of dress than the more successful ones. The relationship between artist and client is one factor, as the expectations of one may not match those of the other. Another factor is whether what is depicted as dress or undress is a reflection of the artist's concerns and wishes, or a record of contemporary tastes for disguise, foreign or exotic styles, or dress for special occasions. There are many permutations that can deceive the unwary, and again, surviving garments can assist in disentangling some of the difficulties, though this is usually applicable to the post-1720 period, due to the relatively small number of earlier survivals. A few of the artists who offered contrasting approaches to the recording of contemporary styles of formal and informal clothing are considered below.

In the late 17th century, as social fluidity and increased wealth offered artists a wider client base, there was still a view that the painter was an artisan or craftsman. If he was as powerful as Sir Peter Lely (1618–80), the most successful portrait painter in the period from 1660 until his death, he could afford studio assistants, provide stock poses, suggest styles of clothing and charge high fees. Other, less well-regarded painters might struggle, unable or unwilling to adapt their style of painting to courtly requirements: the informal shirts, shifts and draperies with which Lely summarized a court which seemed, superficially at least, half-dressed. The supposed 'timelessness' of this approach was much admired in the 18th century and generations of drapery painters made good livings working as assistants to fashionable artists who had many clients and little time to work on a complete portrait. Lely's contemporary John Michael Wright (1617–94) is a useful contrast. He worked occasionally for Charles II and a number of his principal courtiers but many of his clients were on the fringes of, or distanced from, the court circles within which Lely made his fortune. In part this explains the preference of Wright's clients for the type of

39. Studio of Sir Peter Lely, Unknown Woman c. 1670
This is a typical example of the 'undress' that is associated with court portraiture in the post-1660 period. The hairstyle is fashionable and the smock or chemise, the basic female undergarment, is not imagined but the dress appears awkward, the fabric pulled loosely together and pinned just below the décolletage. If this is a nightgown before it is shaped into a mantua it is not a good example. Lely and his studio worked within a certain colour range and this tawny brocaded silk, probably Italian in origin, is typical of his taste for subtlety and the pattern has been softened to almost a blur on certain parts of the garment. This is fashion suborned to artistic needs with the emphasis on the face, upper body and the hands and what they are holding.

40. Caricature, published by H Humphrey, February 1800

The inscription relates this caricature to the Birthday Ball held in January 1800 in honour of Queen Charlotte, the wife of George III, and the carefully delineated face is intended to be immediately recognizable. One of the points so neatly satirized is the disjuncture between the quasi-uniformity of court dress and contemporary male fashions. The hair is cut à la Titus, a style much copied after the French actor Talma wore it on the stage in the 1790s, but the bag and ribbon of a formal court wig are attached to the coat collar. The usual lace cravat worn with the suit sits like frosted decoration below a fashionably high, starched linen cravat and the absurdity is emphasized further by the fuller upper sleeves, the matching fobs, long breeches ties and clocks on the stockings. Both the person, and the event that required a fossilized style of dress, are the butts of the satire.

portraiture that reflected position and wealth through the use of expensive imported silks – brocades, damasks, velvets – fashioned into clothing worn in public or private, with fine jewellery, recognizable fans, gloves, shoes and lace. Occasionally Wright would use a style of garment or a fabric several times, suggesting that he, like Lely, had some studio stock, although this cannot be traced. In contrast, Lely's stock is well documented. After Lely's death the sale of his studio contents included 45 linens and silks of the type seen swathed so casually across or around his sitters: 'Isabella Cloth of Gold' and 'Livered coloured saten' indicate his preferred range of colours from a pale greyish-yellow to a rich red-brown.[4]

Both Lely and Wright were enthusiastic collectors in the manner of a number of their late 17th-century contemporaries. They surrounded themselves with information and materials from old master drawings to contemporary prints, coins and medals. It acted as a source of information for their work but was also not unlike a pension fund, available for sale if times were hard, and Wright did have to sell much of his collection during his lifetime.[5] Wright is interesting to the dress historian in another respect, as he was the son of a tailor. It is perhaps fanciful to attach too much weight to this family craft, but a number of painters, from Van Dyck to Philip de Laszló, also came from backgrounds within which fabric or its construction into garments was a crucial element during their formative years, when the majority of artisans and crafts people lived above or close to their business premises.

Portraiture, although a lucrative and much admired British form of painting well into the early years of the 20th century, vied with other forms such as history painting, genre scenes and landscape. William Hogarth (1697–1764) offers the dress historian almost too much information. His range covered everything from profitable series of engravings based on his own paintings (*The Harlot's Progress, The Rake's Progress, Marriage à la Mode* and *The Election*) to fine group portraits such as those of his servants and the Graham children. He painted individual portraits, notable examples being those of Captain Coram and Miss Mary Edwards. His memorable early painting of *The Beggar's Opera*, which records the proximity of performers to their audience in early 18th-century theatre, was the precursor to a succession of paintings of performers and performances by artists throughout the century.[6] Hogarth's meticulous observation of even the smallest details of dress and undress, etiquette, posture and social customs provide a mine of information for all historians of metropolitan life, including dress historians. Hogarth's sisters Mary and Ann kept a shop in the City of London, which sold ready-to-wear clothing and fabrics; another link between an artist and the clothing trades. Hogarth's work celebrates the social contrasts and volatile nature of life in London, which, by the 1750s, was one of the largest and most powerful cities in Europe. However, there is little sense of a European sensibility or the contemporary interest in foreign travel and the pleasures of disguise, which explored a historical past in masquerades.

A younger artist, Thomas Gainsborough (1727–88) was the son of an East Anglian cloth merchant but his almost impressionistic record of some, though not all, of the clothing he painted does not indicate much interest in that staple English product. He and his contemporary Sir Joshua Reynolds (1723–92) are poles apart in their approach to portraiture, though they had a number of sitters in common. Reynolds spent part of his apprenticeship in Italy and was much influenced by classical sculptures and the great Italian painters of the previous two centuries. His interest in art theory extended to the appropriate styles of dress for his female sitters, his preference being for Greek and Roman styles, '...the simplicity of them consisting of little more than one single piece of drapery without those capricious forms by which all other dresses are embarrassed'. In reality this was translated into a costume with 'the general air of the antique for the sake of dignity' combined with 'something of the modern for the sake of likeness'.[7] The difference between the two artists was summed up by the 20th-century critic Roger Fry: 'Gainsborough never tries to be impressive or noble or dramatic; unlike Reynolds, he has no repertory of artistic devices for making a portrait interesting ... he poses the model in a good light and paints him as he sees him'.[8] Gainsborough rarely reduces fabric to ersatz classical drapery and he also rejected the studio system of assistants that Reynolds used. In a letter to a friend he wrote: 'There is a branch of Painting next in profit to portrait, and quite within your power without anymore drawing than I'll answer for you having, which is Drapery and Landskip backgrounds. Perhaps you don't know that whilst a face painter is harassed to death the drapery painter sits and earns five or six hundred a year, and laughs all the while'.[9]

Here we encounter several problems, which are also found in 17th-century painting: if the 'face' is what the client is paying for are the draperies wholly unreal, even the work of someone else entirely?; do they bear any relationship to contemporary 18th-century dress styles?; are they related to the popularity of masquerades and the reinterpretations of the popular portraits of the 17th century, such as those by Rubens and Van Dyck? Among surviving examples of 18th-century dress there are a few pieces of masquerade costume, just enough to confirm that the costumes were not as historically accurate as Horace Walpole described when he attended a masquerade in 1742: '...quantities of pretty Vandykes, and all kinds of old pictures walked out of their frames'.[10] A surviving 'Vandyke' suit in the collection of Ipswich Museum is self-evidently 18th century in style and construction. It can also be difficult, although not impossible, to identify whether the clothing that an English sitter is wearing in a portrait painted abroad was bought in France or Italy or brought over from England. Rome-based Pompeo Batoni (1708–87) was the most successful Italian artist to paint aristocratic men on the Grand Tour. He painted George Lucy of Charlecote in Warwickshire in 1758, towards the end of Lucy's tour, with the sitter in formal dress of blue velvet coat lavishly embroidered with gold thread, the cuffs of which are silver cloth embroidered with blue and gold to match the waistcoat. Writing home in 1755 when he was in Naples, George Lucy explained that fashionable Italian society: '...dress much and I have been obliged to daub myself all over silver, accompanied by a sword and bag wig'[11]. His grumbles about the formality of Italian clothing help to reinforce the relative simplicity of English dress. This lack of grandeur was noted by foreign visitors to Britain, who found the daytime dress of English men so plain as to cause comment; they were equally confused by the dress of some female servants, which was so rich that it was difficult to ascertain who was mistress and who the servant.

These 18th-century examples indicate some, though far from all, the difficulties encountered by the dress historian when using paintings as a source of information. The pitfalls for the art historian are even greater, as they would be unfamiliar with differing styles of European dress and the use of fabrics, decoration and cut of garments, the conventions about 'real' masquerade costume and imagined draperies. The considerable quantities of clothing of both sexes that survive from about 1720 onwards, though spread between many public and private collections, do provide a valuable additional source for understanding dress in art. However, it is rare to find, outside of publications written by dress historians (Aileen Ribeiro's *The Gallery of Fashion* being an exception), a chronological sequence of portraits discussed in relationship to, and accompanied by, illustrations of dress and accessories.

In the 19th century it is much easier to chart the influence of changing fashions and the impact of movements such as neoclassicism, romanticism, aesthetic dress and dress reform. There is more documentation of artists' ideas about the role and purpose of dress in either historical scenes – there was a passion for attempting to recreate great or imagined moments of history on canvas – or in standard portraits or genre paintings. If artists seemed to be providing a record of their sitters' preferences rather than imposing ideas upon them, what Hazlitt, in discussion of Lawrence's portraits called '...mirrors for personal vanity to contemplate itself in (as you looked in the glass to see how you were dressed)', there were other sitters who invented their own style and burnished it zealously.[12] Lord Byron, the most celebrated author of the early 19th century, was very aware of the power of portraiture and engravings. He knew his best profile, popularized a somewhat raffish elegance of tousled curls, informal shirts and loose or non-existent cravat, and dieted intermittently throughout his short life in order to maintain or sometimes recover a fashionably slender physique. An exhibition held at the National Portrait Gallery in 2003 demonstrated this careful manipulation of what today would be called 'personal image': if Byron was a brand he was hugely influential and the term Byronic is still used long after his poetry is rarely read. Byron was not exactly a dandy, though his interest in his appearance might indicate otherwise, but an artist who was a known dandy was the American James McNeill Whistler (1834–1903).

A recent exhibition and book to commemorate Whistler's centenary, considered not just his career in London and Paris, where he spent most of his working life, but his reputation as a dandy and his profound interest in fashion. His portraits and drawings of women were the subject of the exhibition, along with how he selected his sitters' clothing by even occasionally designing the garments himself. Whistler was interested in aesthetic dress and orientalism but adapted these to form a personal look appropriate for the individual sitter. The exhibition and book were collaborations between art historians and a dress historian, and the mutual benefits of this process can be found throughout the text of *Whistler, Women & Fashion*. The book included examples of surviving costume to demonstrate if and how Whistler edited current styles to suit his vision of his female sitters.

The popularity of genre and history painting in the 19th century is connected to other themes in this book: collecting costume and performance on the stage. Artists, performers and writers often moved in the same circles and discussed their work, each profession influencing the other, sometimes directly, sometimes subliminally. History could cover anything from the ancient world (Greeks and Romans) to the relatively recent past – the French Revolution was much admired in the 1880s and 1890s, not for its politics but as a somewhat romanticized metaphor for recent history. The Revolutionary period, the

Consulate and the First Empire had aroused public interest in Egyptology and paid homage to classical culture. The impact of this interest can be found in everything from dress to architecture. Victorian history painters took whatever suited them from this material and edited it to suit their interests and their public. The painter Marcus Stone (1840–1921) was an artist who enjoyed reinterpreting the period of the French Revolution and its aftermath: one of his favourite paintings, *In Love*, depicts a French soldier and his girlfriend of approximately 1795. Stone had a robust attitude to costume in his work:

> 'The frills and flounces, the cocked hats and long-skirted coats of the time of the French Revolution, are not so unfamiliar to us to-day that we have to draw seriously upon our imaginations to accept as credible the scenes in which they appear, and yet they have about them an atmosphere of picturesqueness which assorts more pleasantly than our own daily dress with love passages and tender ecstasy.'[13]

The idea that the daily dress of 1887–8 was unable to conjure up 'love passages and tender ecstasy' is, of course, nonsense. Stone had found a formula that suited his personal interests and those of the public, whose taste for historical pictures mirrored their taste for historical novels and plays. If Stone limited himself to comparatively recent history, the American artist Edwin Austin Abbey (1852–1911) painstakingly researched his two favourite periods of history, the 15th and 18th centuries. Visitors to his studio were startled to see

'...the amazing wardrobe – an interior building constructed at one end of the studio (in which) hung in due order, classified with such care, love, and pride as an entomologist might display in the arrangement of his specimens, is the vast collection of garments of all periods and styles which Mr. Abbey has collected or had devised, and to which additions are continuously being made. Here they hang, on right and on left, in diminishing perspective...'[14]

Abbey's widow gave some of her husband's collection, which included 18th-century men's and women's clothing and accessories, to the London Museum. This alliance between artists and museums and artists and the theatre (Stone, for example, designed stage costumes for the renowned actress Ellen Terry) was a strong and fruitful one in the second half of the 19th and early 20th centuries.

In 1992 an exhibition entitled The Swagger Portrait was held at the Tate Gallery in London, and in its accompanying catalogue Andrew Wilton argued that 'Grand Manner Portraiture in

41. John Everett Millais, The Nest, 1887
Artists of the 19th century used the dress of previous centuries for everything from dramatic historical paintings to sentimental genre scenes. The sack-back dress worn by the young woman may have been an original garment or especially made by a theatrical costumier. However, the dress and hairstyle pay homage to Ellen Terry's appearance, familiar through engravings and photographs. In the role of Olivia, a part she played from the 1870s well into the 1890s and for which the artist Marcus Stone designed some costumes, she wore sack-back dresses. The little girl's dress is closer to 1800 in style than the earlier hey-day of the sack, which had disappeared by 1780. Like Marcus Stone, Edwin Abbey and Whistler, Millais occasionally designed dresses for his female sitters.

Britain' ended in 1930. In his selection of artists, from John Singer Sargent (1856–1925), believed by some to be the last truly great portrait painter, up to 1930, he included Sir William Orpen (1878–1931), Sir John Lavery (1856–1941), Augustus John (1878–1961) and Philip de László (1869–1937). The clothing in portraits painted by these artists is almost impressionistic, an exploration of colour and line that not only reflects the influence of the artistic trends each painter had absorbed, but is suggestive of, in the female portraits, the freer, more eclectic fashions of the period between c. 1900 and 1914. The 1911 portrait of Lady Rocksavage by Orpen even presents a sitter dressed by Fortuny, that most iconic of early 20th-century dress and textile designers.[15] Although portraits continued to be painted throughout the 20th century and are included in books about 20th-century fashion, they ceded importance to other types of visual record in the post-1914 period.

Prints and photographs

The sheer quantity of printed illustration and, with the introduction of the mezzotint in the late 17th century, its quality, provides another source of information. The printed image was not inexpensive but it was more accessible and covered a much wider range of subject matter than that found in paintings: architecture often with small but distinctively dressed figures to indicate scale; depictions of contemporary events from the popular such as a Frost Fair on the Thames to the flight of a monarch; portraits; ornamental designs and scientific subjects. Many contain information about dress but there was no British equivalent to the work of the French printmakers who, from the early 1670s onwards, were licensed to produce what can be considered the first 'fashion plates'. These depict men and women in black and white or colour and were an elegant advertisement for the luxury trades of France – silks, lace, accessories, new styles of dress – that prospered under the careful supervision of Louis XIV's Controller-General of Finance, Jean Baptiste Colbert. They were eagerly collected (both John Evelyn and Samuel Pepys owned groups of them) and a few English versions based on the French models seem to have been made. They were also a source for figures in prints of contemporary events. However the most successful adaptation of a French prototype was *The Cryes of London Drawne after the Life*, the work of Marcellus Laroon, which was engraved and then published by Pierce Tempest. The complete set of 74 images was completed by the summer of 1689 and depicts a variety of trades and individuals with or without distinctive cries. Pepys's annotations indicate that they show known persons and were not purely decorative. A set was bought for 12 shillings in 1692, a modest outlay compared to a portrait.[16]

In the 18th century collections of prints could be supplemented with pocket books and periodicals; the last two included small prints, usually in black and white, depicting court occasions, named people, and new styles accompanied by detailed descriptions of fashions, fabrics, accessories and jewellery. As the market for these illustrations grew throughout Europe a good deal of copying took place, and by the late 18th century fine examples of the work of such well-known artists as Heideloff were circulating in pirated form with only a change of language to suit a new readership.[17] Within the journals such as *Ackermann's Repository* (1809–1829) plates sometimes had small examples of fabric or advertised makers of the styles illustrated, replacing the fashion doll as the provider of information about the

42. Fashion plate from Le Beau Monde, *July 1807; photograph by John Chase*

One of the frustrations of fashion plates is that they often separate the sexes. This becomes increasingly noticeable in the course of the 19th century. Therefore a plate like this which depicts a couple is useful evidence of what was considered the appropriate dress for both sexes during a particular season or time of day. The man's trousers were a newly acceptable alternative to breeches as daywear, a style appropriated from the trousers worn by working men, sailors and soldiers. This is an example of a type of garment moving up the social structure.

latest female fashions. The plates, until the demise of Ackermann's in 1829, were mostly hand-coloured and like earlier prints much collected. Many plates have, unfortunately, been removed from the magazines and lack the original details; there was a vogue for producing books of these prints later in the 19th century, a species of pretty scrap-album of past fashions.

The idealized prettiness of the prints (no-one is old, or fat, or ugly) is one of many reasons to use this evidence with caution; these fashions were undoubtedly adapted or simplified but certainly never looked so appealing on the spectrum of human physiognomies that emulated them. Female fashion plates had a wider and more appreciative audience than those for male fashions, especially so in the 19th century when, so we have been led to believe, male fashions became rather less flamboyant. A notable exception to the idea that only female fashions were regularly illustrated can be found in the prints published by Benjamin Read in the period between c. 1825 and c. 1848. Read was a tailor as well as a publisher and obviously recognized the advertising potential of visual depictions of his craft. He sold the plates to subscribers but also wrote books on tailoring and probably found a market among provincial tailors. The plates are large and use a recognizable London location as a backdrop, with a frieze of fashionably dressed men and women and a few children massed at the front rather in the manner of a staged performance. Can it be coincidence that the highly popular juvenile play sheets were appearing at much the same time? In the manner of all successful entrepreneurs Read emphasized his unique selling point: men's tailoring. The male figures are shown from all angles – front, three-quarters and behind – so that the cut and fit of the garments can be admired, and every type of garment, from formal evening wear to riding habits, is illustrated. They are colourful and their female companions and the children are a foil to the masculine tailoring.[18] Others produced similar plates to Read and they all competed with the *Gentlemen's Magazine of Fashion, Fancy Costumes, and the Regimentals of the Army*, which appeared from 1829 to 1850 and, as its title indicates, covered every type of male clothing.

Magazines of this sort, aimed at a male market, were a sideshow in the march of ever-increasing numbers of women's magazines in Europe and North America. Such magazines had a varied content, with a mixture of the practical – housekeeping tips, how to crochet, knit or embroider anything from a cushion to the Berlin wool-work men's slippers which were such popular presents – to hints on etiquette and discussions of the latest fashions. They also provided a living for many women who wrote columns and short stories, designed the practical patterns and offered the housekeeping tips. The idea that they are purely about women's domestic concerns is being quashed; they provided a forum not merely an amusement, and clothing is just one element in this complex world of female achievement. It was the depictions of fashion that intrigued collectors of fashion plates and magazines for women, and some of the most significant collectors were men, including Herbert Druitt, C W Cunnington, Sir Basil Liddell Hart and Harry Matthews. All are now in the public domain, one in the south-west, two in the north and one in London, giving a useful national spread. These are in addition to other collections that are not known by the names of their collectors and are therefore more institutional, having been assembled by generations of curators whose interests may, quite reasonably, have had more to do with the techniques of print-making than the actual image contained within the print.

These public and private collections also contain caricatures and cartoons, the satirical record of the fashionable foibles of both sexes. In many the clothing is decoration: the satire is political or social. In others the absorption of both sexes in trying to look younger, thinner or ultra-fashionable is satirized mercilessly. Caricature can be broadly based – poking fun at a group – or cruelly personal in targeting individuals. They add excitement to discussion of dress but they cannot be viewed as other than a wicked over-emphasis of aspects of life that appealed to artists who specialized in this genre. After it was discovered in the 1830s, photography became the popular medium for recording people and places, and remained so over the next 60 years until early films captivated audiences with movement. From the beginnings of photography a few people treated it reverentially, as if it might be a type of art, but the artist Alfred Chalon confidently replied to Queen Victoria that it was no threat to his livelihood because it could not flatter the sitter. This was gradually disproved as equipment and photographic skill improved, but for much of the century the technical process of transferring photographic images onto engraved plates in order to illustrate newspapers and magazines was rarely attempted. The black and white process was also limiting, although some photographs were laboriously and unconvincingly hand-tinted.

The importance of photography lay in the fact that it was inexpensive and reasonably fast. The pleasure of recording a place, person or event by this method soon ensured that many people took it up as a hobby. It is impossible to estimate the number of photographic prints that survive, not from the early period but from about 1870 onwards: libraries, museums and families own, in total, many millions. The postcard format was particularly successful and many millions were produced, depicting people and events. The combined total of the material that remains, in the form of photographs, postcards and negatives, provides a much wider range of evidence about the social circumstances, occupations and age of, and the clothing worn by, the figures in them. Yet, like all forms of visual evidence, their content can be selective or calculated. The intentions of the photographer, the market for 'commercial' subjects and the expectations of the sitter are not easy to interpret. Many of the images are not annotated; there is no date, no name of sitter and no intimation as to why and how the image was made. However, the existence of this additional category of information is of considerable use to the dress historian alongside other complementary sources. In museums that collect dress the donation of a garment is given an additional meaning if it is accompanied by a photograph of the original wearer, a date, some indication of the person's social circumstances and the occasions on which the garment was worn.

Dress and fashion as art

The double-negative quote at the head of this chapter by André Courrèges, in regard to the question of whether fashion was an art, was more circumspect than many have suggested both before and after him. The term art was used to describe dress in the 19th century, indeed *The Art of Dress* by Mrs H R Haweis was published in 1879. Mrs Haweis was both a dress historian and commentator on contemporary styles of dress and she is particularly associated with ideas of aesthetic dress and dress reform. Dress reform was a

43. Dress and jacket by Mariano Fortuny, Venice 1920
This pleated silk Delphos dress has drawstrings edged with glass beads. The jacket is of printed velvet, gold on black, and the lining is of red ribbed silk. Fortuny (1871–1949) was Spanish, and grew up in an environment of collecting: his parents collected antique textiles, as did his maternal uncle. He trained as an artist and worked on theatrical projects in the 1890s. The influence of Renaissance and classical art can be discerned in these two garments, though his tastes were eclectic and he found inspiration from many cultures and continents. He patented the Delphos pleating technique and the design of the dress in Paris in 1909. Characteristics of his work include his painterly approach to colours and his use of printing on luxurious fabrics.
(By courtesy, V&A Picture Library)

44. Detail from an evening dress, English c. 1925
Topicality or rather fashion responding to events
related to the historic past can be observed in this
detail of beaded griffins and pyramids on a cream
silk crepe dress. The discovery of the tomb of
Tutankhamun in 1922 heralded a range of Egyptian
motifs on everything from cinema facades to items
of clothing.

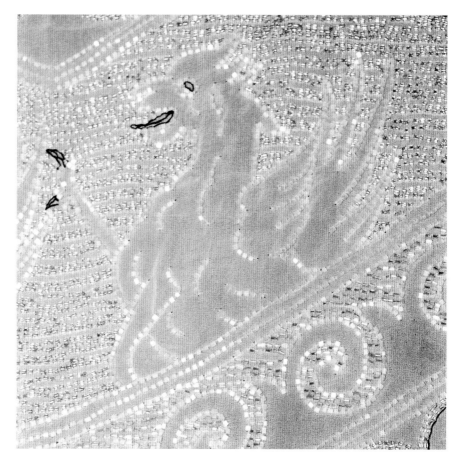

subject that rumbled on for much of the second half of the 19th century but was of particular concern in the 1870s and 1880s. Admiration of the art of the past, whether Greek or medieval, was an aspect of the discussion of the most 'artistic' styles of women's dress. E W Godwin, whom we encountered in the context of the short-lived Costume Society of 1882–3, gave a lecture at the time of the International Health Exhibition of 1884 in which he told his audience: 'As Architecture is the art and science of building, so Dress is the art and science of clothing ... Where art is a living reality with peoples, their costumes will be the first to declare it ...'.[19] This idea was not universally acceptable, as shown in the preface to Talbot Hughes's book on *Dress Design*, written by the series editor: 'The designing and making of Costume is a craft – sometimes artistic – with which we are all more or less concerned. It is also, in its own way, one of the living arts, that is, it is still carried forward experimentally by experts directly attached to the "business"'.[20] The idea of a 'living art' as opposed to a living craft is one that appealed to the designer Elsa Schiaparelli. Her view of her work was that it was 'a most difficult and unsatisfactory art, because as soon as a dress is born it has already become a thing of the past'.[21] This idea that dress or fashion is an ephemeral art, if indeed it is an art at all, permeated 20th-century approaches to how it was discussed, recorded and presented, and is especially pertinent to the dress of the past as written about and collected. 'The art of costume' is discussed in an article in *Vogue* in 1920, which describes an exhibition of historic dress held in Paris in that year. In somewhat florid language the author Albert Depréaux describes fashion as 'the history of civilization, and often the most impressive commentary of its philosophy, so intimately bound together that to detach the life of a people from their costume and their ornaments is to neglect one of the most vital forces of the past'.[22]

This idea found similar expression in America when the Museum of Costume Art, the precursor of the Costume Institute, was initiated in 1937. Polaire Weissman, the first Executive Director of the Museum and later of the Institute, presented an exhibition at the Metropolitan in 1967 called The Art of Fashion. In an essay she noted that, 'Fashion in costume documents the taste of its time in the same manner as do painting, sculpture, and other works of art...', and later, 'The art of fashion is so intrinsically woven into the fabric of the story of man that one can hardly be separated from the other'.[23] The idea that both the dress of the past and current fashions was art gradually took root, but there were obvious doubters. Thomas Hoving, Director of the Metropolitan, declared in 1971: '...costumes have seldom been thought of as works of art in their own right. The belief that they *are* art led the Metropolitan to take the Museum of Costume Art under its roof in 1946 ...'.[24] If repeated regularly enough an idea can gain acceptance and both books and exhibitions began to use the term art with carefree abandon, resulting in *The Art of Fashion* 1600–1939 (Victoria & Albert Museum booklet, 1978), *An Elegant Art, Fashion and Fantasy in the Eighteenth Century* (exhibition and catalogue, Los Angeles County Museum, 1983) and *The Art of Dress, Clothes and Society* 1500–1914 (National Trust book, 1996) to name just a few.

Within institutions that had collected textiles, sometimes including dress because the textile was an important or unusual one, the shift was no less apparent. In 1988 the Whitworth Art Gallery in Manchester produced a book to commemorate its centenary. The first Governors had decided that one of their aims must be to form a collection of textiles as a source of inspiration for the northern textile industries. They commissioned tapestries and bought the collection of Sir Charles Robinson, which contained fine early embroideries, fabrics and vestments in 1891.[25] The Gallery became a department of Manchester University in 1958 and in 1968 early textiles transferred from the Manchester Museum further enhanced its collection.[26] So by the time of its centenary publication, in which it described the range of its several departments and chose to illustrate and describe *60 works of art* [my italics] from the collection, it chose 14 textile examples ranging in date from a 4th-century AD embroidered Coptic panel to a Collier and Campbell furnishing fabric of 1982. Within this group were three items that might be described as dress: a Spanish funeral cope of the mid-16th century, an Indian dyed and painted cotton petticoat of c. 1750–75 and a Brussels *point de gaze* lace collar of c. 1860–70. All three items are described as more than merely technically interesting textiles and their use is explained, but only the cope is displayed as a garment in the photographs. Changes in attitudes occur within all institutions and by 2003 there was a display of both flat textiles and costumed figures offering a vivid summary, in terms of colour, design and pattern, of an impressive range: Coptic dress, vestments, English domestic embroidery, arts and crafts movement textiles, Indian brocades, Chinese Imperial costume, West African textiles, European folk

45. (right) Coat-dress by Bill Gibb, 1972; photograph by John Chase
This cream rayon coat-dress with gored full skirt is fastened with metallic buttons in the shape of bumble-bees. The seams are top-stitched in yellow and black thread and its label states 'Bill Gibb, London. Size 10'. Talented designers absorb the ideas of the past and express them in their own manner, in the fabrics and colours and details available within the period in which they work. However, at a quick glance, the similarity between this coat-dress and the pelisse suggest one source of inspiration.

46. (far right) Pelisse c. 1810; photograph by John Chase
This item is made from cotton with the wide collar formed from four widths of scallop-edged Broderie Anglaise. The centre-front fastening is by three covered buttons.

dress, contemporary knitting and a section devoted to cotton prints from Manchester produced for the East and West African market.

Given this new perception that dress/fashion might be an art, which is partly due to a blurring between craft and art as 20th-century artists moved between the two, it was perhaps inevitable that a major exhibition held at the Hayward Gallery in London from autumn 1998 to early 1999 would be called Addressing the Century, 100 Years of Art & Fashion. It was potentially an interesting idea and, as the booklet that accompanied the exhibition indicated, its purpose was to explore the relationships between fashion designers and artists working separately or together, sometimes annexing each other's ideas and roles. It considered new technology and its impact, including film, photography and video alongside works of art, drawings by artists and designers interested in dress, and clothing actually worn or created as an experimental use of materials that exaggerated or played with the boundaries of the viewers' perceptions of art and fashion. However, it could not and did not offer an historical survey or make the case for fashion as art, as noted in the preface to the catalogue that accompanied the exhibition.[27] Looking again at the selection of artefacts, reading the essays and a review of the exhibition we are reminded of what was missing and how unsympathetic the design of the spaces and displays were. Perhaps that was intentional and reflects one of the ideas contained in an essay by Elizabeth Wilson and Joanne Entwistle: 'Dress, the body and the self constitute a totality, and when dress and body are pulled apart, as in the costume museum, we grasp only a fragment, a partial snapshot of dress, our understanding limited'[28]. Later in the essay, the importance of these museum displays is acknowledged because they are 'art/craft objects in their own right' but also because they '...reveal their incompleteness when withdrawn from the body'.[29]

Does this assist understanding of whether 20th-century dress/fashion is an art? In some ways it does. Those working within a specialist costume museum or a museum in which costume is curated among other collections can continue to display and interpret their collections in many different ways, assisted by many more types of supplementary evidence. If they wish to present 20th-century fashion as an art, this may irritate art critics but at least it makes them reconsider the blurring of ideas about where art begins and craft ends. Perhaps the sheer expense of couture garments (it is regularly said that there are only about 300 women in the world who can afford to buy couture and nothing else) is an indication that buying fashion can be more costly than buying works of art. This, of course, is not new. Clothing was expensive in previous centuries but principally because the fabrics and the decoration used on it were costly. This has been replaced by the rise of the named couturier or designer, no longer a nameless artisan but a creative artist whose signature – the label within the garment – guarantees originality. The label or the logo has assumed a power that transcends its associated status. The hushed reverence afforded to Fortuny, Chanel, Schiaparelli, Dior and Balenciaga is summarized by a tiny label, which no-one can see but without which a garment loses credibility. Recently an evening coat attributed to Paul Poiret was auctioned but, because it lacked his label, was acquired for a fraction of the price it might have reached with its label.[30] In that sense, if none other, fashion since the introduction of the label is wholly similar to art: the signature and provenance are of paramount importance to the original and subsequent purchasers. Those outside museums can fit dress/fashion into any number of disciplines, but this does not help the student who wants to understand the role of fashion in the 20th century. Assessing the evidence that has amassed since the couturier/fashion designer escaped from anonymity and became a known brand, a celebrity as famous as those they dress, is far from easy. Bibliographies, those sturdy standbys mentioned in an earlier chapter, list the widest variety of source material: newspaper and magazine archives, designer archives, biographies, autobiographies, fashions by decade or period, works on everything from accessories to in-depth studies of one designer and exhibition catalogues. They also list more recent work by writers who examine ordinary patterns of consumption, such as ready-to-wear and inexpensive brands, which may or may not have been influenced by the seminal names and movements of art and fashion. Looking at 20th-century fashion in museums can be equally confusing if, indeed, there is a representative group on display. The opportunities to compare and contrast the work of several designers working as contemporaries can be informative, but the modern emphasis on presenting the work of just one designer, dead or living, often eliminates this critical option. Gauging the originality or the derivative nature of modern fashion designers is occasionally assisted by one of them speaking frankly. Zandra Rhodes, interviewed in May 2003 at the opening of

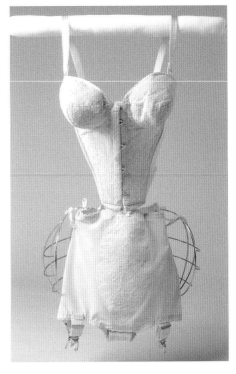

47. Corset and cage bustle, 1994; photograph by John Chase
This size 10 boned nylon corset has a padded bust, detachable shoulder straps and centre front hook fastening. The bustle is of wire sprayed gold with a shaped waist. Both pieces are part of Vivienne Westwood's Erotic Zones Collection; the corset has a label 'Vivienne Westwood, London Made in England'. An immensely influential designer, Westwood's work has drawn inspiration from sub-cultures and historical sources and she has been constantly innovative in her approach to fashion across several decades.

her new Fashion and Textile Museum in London, was refreshingly honest: 'All designers are endowed with two or three great ideas and if they return once more, we are very fortunate'.[31] She was equally frank about why she formed the museum: 'I bought this place in 1996 because my work was being ignored, and I felt I should donate it to the nation so I wouldn't be forgotten'.[32] Her personal archive contains 3000 items dating back to 1968 and is balanced by the work, though not in the same quantity, of other designers. It will be a useful resource for fashion and textile design students but if the museum is to survive, to ensure that she is not forgotten, it will have to place her within fashion history. Other museums, however much she may not feel in step with their selective approach to collecting, have both the collections and critical skills to provide this context for her work and that of her contemporaries.

Another difficulty when considering whether fashion is art or something much more changeable, depending upon the actual designs and clothing under scrutiny, is the 'missing man'. This is shorthand for where menswear generally, and tailoring specifically, fit in to discussions on dress in the 20th century. There are relatively few books and exhibitions that have analyzed and interpreted men's clothes after 1900. Is this indicative of a lack of interest in this area, a reinforcement of the idea of the 'Great Masculine Renunciation'? Admittedly there are modern magazines for men that discuss clothing, and academic journals and collections of essays often include one or more contributions on an aspect of male clothing, but the list of recent publications is slight compared to the shelves of work on women and fashion. Male curators and trained dress historians are less active in this area than their academic counterparts. The ranks of fashion designers, fashion photographers and fashion journalists contain many influential men but their principal audience is women. The interpretation of the history of dress/fashion shifted in the 20th century from being primarily a male area of study to a female one. It was only when the emphasis in menswear moved from elite styles of male dress to counter-cultural and cross-disciplinary influences that male academics, sociologists and others, began to show renewed interest in fashion. If we return, briefly, to the exhibition Addressing the Century: 100 Years of Art & Fashion, it hardly discussed men except as artists, designers, film-makers and photographers of fashion for women. This might be perceived as a backhanded compliment, but it leaves a gap in our knowledge of the 20th century; we know little about men's engagement with fashion and their views on whether what they wear is an art or an ephemeral but distinguished craft.

48. Labels authenticating the clothing of the post-1870 period
In the manner of a signed painting, these labels offer provenance of the couturier, dressmaker, fashion designer or shop from which the garment was originally purchased: Madame Clapham c. 1895; Jean Doucet c. 1890–95; Jeanne Lanvin c. 1935; André Courrèges c. 1969; Zandra Rhodes c. 1968–9; Vivienne Westwood, from the Erotic Zones Collection, 1994.

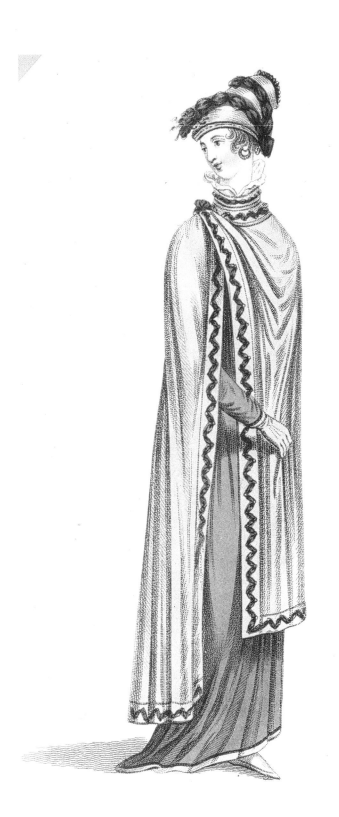

49. *Fashion plate from* La Belle Assemblée, *January 1811; photograph by John Chase*
The woman's carriage dress, though eminently fashionable, is not wholly dissimilar in its decoration to the short-lived French experiment with a mantle designed for French Deputies in 1797–8. This type of elision between uniform and fashion is not unusual.

6 Uniformity and disguise

'An interesting blend of conscious archaism and contemporary fashion'. John Nevinson[1]

Although certain areas of dress appear to be tangential to the processes of production and consumption that result in fashion, they are, nevertheless, far from insignificant. It can be argued that all clothing, to a greater or lesser extent, offers either uniformity or disguise. Disappearing into an undifferentiated mass of people is relatively easy if social conventions require this, although human ingenuity often prevails and some individuality shines through. The reverse of this, the desire to be different or innovative, may indicate powerful personalities and the intellectual or financial means to explore boundaries (the exotic, the foreign, the historical), or it might just suggest eccentricity. Outlined in this chapter are a group of topics for which there are surviving garments and documentary and published evidence, to offer students another perspective on how fashion absorbs techniques from unlikely sources and how the dress of the past is used as an interpretive tool.

Uniform has a number of dictionary definitions. One, dating back to 1748, states: 'A distinctive dress of uniform materials, colour, and cut, worn by all the members of a particular military, naval, or other force to which it is recognized properly belonging and peculiar'. A secondary definition of 1837 is also pertinent: 'A distinctive uniform dress worn by members of any civilian body or association of persons'. A further definition, first found in 1550, is even more telling, though it has little to do with clothing (or does it?): 'Having or presenting the same appearance or aspect; hence, having a plain, unbroken, or undiversified surface or exterior'. In a dictionary of synonyms we can progress further still: replacement nouns for uniform include 'costume, dress, outfit, regalia, livery'. This encompasses almost every topic discussed in this book but also makes sense of the diversity contained within this chapter.

Uniformity

If we consider the idea of something or somebody 'having or presenting the same appearance or aspect', this creates a discussion about whether, in the period from 1660 onwards, the growth in distinctive uniforms is separate from, or influenced by, economic and gender-imposed uniformity, both of which could be interpreted as suppressing individuality. 'Economic and gender uniformity' is an inelegant shorthand for the obvious fact that the majority of any country's population wore locally produced fabrics, home tailored into sturdy basic garments suited to varying forms of hard daily labour and indicative of their gender. An obvious exception to this sweeping generalization is regional folk dress and national costumes, which do, from time to time, have an impact on fashionable dress, but although these are important they are beyond the remit of this book. However, given that caveat, most men and women in western countries were differentiated by their clothing in the most basic way: men wore breeches or trousers and women did not.

All small boys wore skirts until they were between five and seven (this varies according to century), the age at which they could begin their education apart from their female siblings. So the exhibition, Men in Skirts, held at the Costume Institute of the Metropolitan Museum, New York in 2003, was exploring a phenomenon with a lengthy history.

What was unacceptable was female adoption of breeches; everyone knew that women had legs but only artists' models and cross-dressing actresses, both considered socially dubious, were actually allowed to show them. The constrictions and restrictions placed on female clothing reflect the Judeo-Christian view of women as both inferior to men but, like Eve, capable of leading them astray by overt displays of various parts of their anatomies, including their legs. So, to put it quite simply, until the late 19th century, men could wear 'skirts' and trousers, but women were subject to criticism whenever any aspect of their appearance suggested masculinity, like short hair, a jacket, breeches, trousers. This did not, of course, prevent some adventurous women joining the army or navy, becoming pirates or adopting a male role in civilian life, but they are comparatively rare. So, whatever the economic circumstances of the individual, s/he was usually recognizable due to the social conventions surrounding how s/he was expected to dress.

The collapse of this distinctive uniformity had its origins in the 19th century but, in the words of C W Cunnington in *English Women's Clothing in the Nineteenth Century*, 'Already, in [18]'51, an American lady, Mrs Bloomer, had demanded that her sex should be allowed to wear trousers, an extreme measure which received no sympathy in this country ...'[2] In his later companion volume, *English Women's Clothing in the Present Century*, which describes the evolution of female clothing from 1900 to 1950, he was still unsure about women and trousers: 'Among the many innovations which have been introduced is the wearing of man's own garment, trousers, or indeed his complete suit. It required a Great War to break the "trouser taboo", and even to-day a certain prejudice lingers'.[3] The book was published in 1953 when the country was accustomed to seeing its young queen photographed informally in tailored riding jacket and jodhpurs, though during the ceremonial of the Trooping the Colour the same young woman in scarlet uniform jacket wore the traditional skirt for riding side saddle. This odd double standard about when and where women's trousers were acceptable persisted in some professions until quite recently, usually, though not always, enforced by men.

Fifty years on from 1953 it is likely that many women in western countries own more pairs of trousers than skirts and, probably, more pairs of trousers than are found in the wardrobes of their male colleagues, friends and relatives. Men are more reticent about skirts, excluding dressing gowns and kaftans, and even the latter are usually worn only by the supremely self-confident. Within a multicultural society knowledge of the traditional male forms of dress of African, Near Eastern and Asian countries, which have evolved to suit both climate and cultural circumstances, is a visual given but rarely imitated. The Scottish kilt is one of the few examples of a type of garment associated with a skirt that western men are prepared to wear in public, and it is occasionally parodied by eccentric fashion designers, actors and pop stars. David Beckham in a sarong and Samuel L Jackson in a kilt do not herald a movement towards men in skirts. The legs of western men, when revealed in heat waves or on holiday, are ill prepared for such exposure. Sportsmen, whose

*50. Woman's Spencer c. 1820–23 (front and back
views); photographs by John Chase*
*Within the confines of this silk taffeta, hand-sewn
garment, which was worn over a day dress, homage
is paid to a number of historical and contemporary
influences. The clusters of decorative petal-like
shapes around the neck and at the top of the
sleeves are known as Vandyking, supposedly after the
17th-century Flemish artist, but more akin to the
quasi-17th-century styles worn on the stage or as
masquerade costumes in the 18th century. Historical
features, such as Medici collars and Mary Stuart
caps, record the delight in historical and romantic
subject matter found in painting and on clothing in
the first decades of the 19th century. The applied
bands of rouleau ribbons set diagonally on the front
and back of the Spencer hint at military uniform, as
do the bands of imitation braiding on the outer arm.
Decorative features and/or distinctive colours derived
from military or naval uniforms were regularly
plundered and adapted for fashionable wear.*

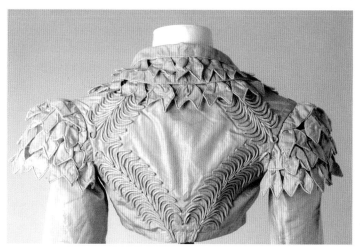

muscular limbs are regularly paraded in shorts, are the exception to this rule. Trousers or leg coverings were associated with barbarians by the Greeks and Romans. The latter lived in a climate that allowed their bodies to appear natural in short tunics, but even they had monstrous full-length ceremonial garments in which they enveloped themselves on formal occasions. Being a pragmatic people the Romans accepted the need for leg-coverings or trousers when in colder climates, but retained tunics and togas until comparatively late during the empire's history. More recently, in the period covered by this book, familiarity with closer-fitting leg coverings (breeches and trousers) and their functionality, have relegated male skirts to an amusing diversion rather than a viable alternative.

In contemporary western culture, commentators deride the idea of uniformity of appearance by telling us that we live in a world of boundless personal choice. The ultimate statement of individuality should, but rarely does, find its expression in clothing. The construction of personal appearance owes much to cultural and social conditioning. It is not necessary to subscribe to Jean Baudrillard's ideas about there being no reality or originality, only simulations formed by the media images with which we are surrounded. It is dress codes, peer group pressures, the clothing available in the shops that inform how we decide to dress. The uncertain buy books on how to make themselves over, or their friends subject them to the ritual humiliation of being televised and criticized by self-appointed stylists like Susannah Constantine and Trinny Woodall who offer, to a degree, a simulation, a mediated view of how to dress. Their approach is fashion-centred and ignores individuality, but is based upon a long tradition of books, magazines and articles on etiquette and dress that counsel the socially or physically insecure, thus ensuring that they conform to the uniformity of the period. Individuality in appearance is often perceived as eccentricity and most people of all ages, genders or cultures can be recognized by the badges of their peer group, such as Barbours, Levis, customized baseball caps, hooded fleeces. These are not language but are a visual symbol of inclusiveness, which, even if spurious and temporary, indicates a wish for some form of uniformity.

Uniforms and occupational dress

The idea of a distinctive style of clothing being associated with an occupation has a history that reaches back much further than 1660. Social stratification and economic dependency offer two basic reasons for the provision of clothing by elite groups in society to those who served them. Among a number of dictionary definitions for the word 'livery' is one that is pertinent here: 'A distinctive suit or badge bestowed by a person upon his retainers or servants; a distinctive badge or suit worn by a servant or official, a member of a company etc.' Providing fabric and/or made garments was both part-payment and a method of ensuring a degree of uniformity in appearance among servants, soldiers, sailors and other groups who lived within a communal and hierarchical system. By the 19th century it extended to schoolchildren, nurses, policemen and felons in prison, but its most florid expression was always found in the design of military uniforms. The many surviving portraits and, particularly in European collections, the actual uniforms themselves, provide stunning visual evidence of this colourful and expensive excess. Generally speaking, uniforms worn by the armed forces are kept in specialist museums and curated by those

Uniformity and disguise □

with expertise in the complexities of their design and manufacture, and there is a large and comprehensive literature devoted to this subject.

However, the significance of uniforms in a book that explains the evolution of fashion goes much beyond the bewildering quantity and range. Distinctive colours, sashes and styles had begun to evolve in the 17th century, but a complete uniform is an 18th-century innovation, and it is no accident that the development of men's tailoring later in the 18th and into the 19th centuries ran in parallel with the sophisticated tailoring of uniforms. When London became renowned for the expertise in and quality of its men's tailoring it owed a good deal to the skills of those originally trained as military tailors in Germany. Such men transferred their expertise to the requirements of demanding customers like Beau Brummell, the Prince Regent and their circle in the late 18th and early 19th centuries.[4] Aspects of dress associated with soldiers also percolated through into non-military fashions. The Steinkerk cravats of the 1690s were named after the battle of 1692, and the fashionable Hussar braiding in the 18th century expressed admiration of the Hungarian Hussars who had made a lasting impression with their bravery at the battle of Dettingen in 1743. The painter Arthur Devis had a miniature hussar suit for use on the lay figure in his studio, and the battle of Dettingen was one of the spectacles of fairground theatre in the late 1740s.[5]

51. Cartoon from Punch *magazine, 1852*
Throughout its history Punch *cartoonists enjoyed poking fun at what it perceived as absurd styles of dress. Here a group of women, in exaggerated skirts and 'Bloomers' are depicted behaving like young men in a bar, smoking pipes and cheroots and planning an evening at the Haymarket Theatre. The young women's short, wide skirts are similar to those worn by professional dancers but, in fact, the Haymarket, under the management of the actor and dramatist Benjamin Webster, was noted for its respectability and high standards of performance. In 1852 the comedy* Masks and Faces, *set in the 18th-century world of the theatre, was the great success. In a nuanced image* Punch *may be associating the young women with actresses playing roles.*

SOMETHING MORE APROPOS OF BLOOMERISM.
(BEHIND THE COUNTER THERE IS ONE OF THE "INFERIOR ANIMALS.")

52. Detail from girl's dress c. 1895–1900
The smocking, embroidery and delicate fabric are
wholly removed from the original practicality of the
working smock.

53. Photograph of Samuel Sinfield (died 1904)
From the late 18th century many farm workers in the
South of England and the Midlands wore smocks or
Round Frocks. The distinctive embroidery had
appeared by the 1830s. Smocks could be made at
home or bought from shops, were made of linen and
twilled cotton and were loose enough to be worn
over a jacket. There is a carefully posed artfulness
about this photograph in which both the sitter and
the unknown photographer appear to be conspiring.

Uniformity and disguise □

Designing uniforms became a popular pastime for British monarchs. George III introduced the Windsor Uniform for his closest circle in the late 1770s and his son, the Prince Regent, later George IV, was at his sunniest designing uniforms for himself, his household, including public servants, and his regiments.[6] The Italian war of 1859 popularized the Zouave jacket for men and women, which was based on the garment worn by the Algerian-French Zouave troops. British women lionized the Italian freedom fighter Garibaldi by adapting his red shirts in the early 1860s. Naval-style jackets were worn by women in the 1870s and small boys paraded in miniature naval whites. The colour navy blue quickly outgrew its seafaring connotations. In the 20th century a number of changes in uniforms, for instance the blouson-style jacket and the duffel coat, found their way into the visual repertory of fashion. Young men and women raided army surplus stores in the 1960s and 1970s for greatcoats and leather flying jackets, and the ubiquity of camouflage fabric in the late 20th century is so usual as to be unremarkable. These are such potentially fruitful areas of study that it is surprising that few curators who work with uniforms or the clothing inspired by them have examined the continuing dialogue between the two areas.

It is probable that uniforms of the armed services survive in greater numbers than do other garments worn by the majority of the working population. Some of the more extravagant styles of servant's uniforms survive, but these are atypical. The widest range of distinctive styles of occupational clothing – uniform of a sort – can be glimpsed in paintings, prints and drawings, but there are few groups of survivals until the 19th century. Any surviving garments are often associated with a region or an activity, such as collections of smocks. Avril Lansdell's article, 'A Guide to the Study of Occupational Costume in the Museums of England and Wales', recorded items of occupational clothing in 1971, a type of research that is still rare.[7] She listed items held by 83 museums and gave an analysis of the 51 occupations represented, but the latter places much emphasis, in the category of farmers and farm workers, on smocks: farm labourers' smocks, a beekeeper's smock, carters' smocks and shepherds' smocks. She provided an additional list of the 60 out of the 83 museums that held examples of smocks.

In part this fascination with smocks owes much to the evolution of folk-life studies and the setting up of folk-life museums, or special collections within museums that pre-dated a later shift towards industrial archaeology and rather less romantic styles of working clothing. It is this skewing of the evidence that often suggests to academic scholars of dress that survivals are a matter of curatorial whim rather than clear-sighted collecting policies, although the smock certainly provides yet another example of 'men in skirts' well beyond the fashionable mainstream. It also inspired emulation among women who favoured aesthetic dress. In 1880 it was noted that: 'No artistic dresser would be without a Smock cut exactly like a farm labourer's, with square turned-down collar, gatherings front and back, gathered full sleeves, worn over a habit shirt, and looped up over an under-skirt with a belt at the waist.[8] Smocks and smocking became idealized symbols of simplicity and honest labour, and generations of children with circumstances far removed from toiling on the land, wore miniature versions of the garment itself or clothes decorated with smocking.

The prescribed or traditional garments of occupational dress have been discussed in articles and displayed, when they survive, as an adjunct to local crafts and trades, but this is yet another under-researched area. It would be feasible to approach the subject from numerous angles and it fits neatly into categories such as gender studies, cultural history and mainstream discussion of dress and textiles. The economics of manufacture and distribution also offer possibilities for research. An obvious starting point is why uniforms, both prescribed and occupational, are so pervasive at all levels in society. John Harvey's book *Men in Black* provides a good example of intelligent lateral thinking about men's clothing and the degree to which black as an expensive dye, a symbol of rectitude and sobriety but a colour which also copes with grubby environmental conditions, offered a type of uniformity throughout the period discussed in this book.

Ceremonial dress

This is a wide category and can be defined in a variety of ways. Usually it includes the formal dress worn at European courts, at major events such as coronations, robes connected with orders of chivalry, the garments designed or accidentally developed to render lawyers and academics imposing in appearance and the dress of the clergy. The common element is the fossilization of dress and, for much of the period under review; its specific application is to the clothing of men. Naturally women played a part in the life of royal courts and the special events surrounding them. Elite groups are sometimes ignored because they are atypical and too closely associated with traditional forms of dress history, but the exquisite pomposity and absurdities of correct dress and insignia offer both instruction and amusement. Even in modern democracies it is accepted that certain events are rendered more impressive by the use of fossilized styles of dress.

One interesting aspect of some types of ceremonial dress that fall within the period of this book is that they were consciously devised to (re)create a sense of the historical past, misunderstood perhaps, but important to those involved in their promulgation. When Charles II was restored to the throne in 1660 he took a particular interest in reconstituting the Order of the Garter, a select chivalric band of 24 members selected by the monarch. It was his decision that the underdress '...followed too much the modern fashion, never constant and less comporting with the decency, gravity, and stateliness of the upper Robes of the Order', and determined upon a uniform style of a short doublet and '...the old trunk-hose or round breeches'.[9] John Nevinson, after examining the underdress on the effigy of Charles II in Westminster Abbey in the 1930s, described these garments as '...an interesting blend of conscious archaism and contemporary fashion, at a time when little was known of the history of dress'.[10] In fact the 'conscious archaism' had less to do with the history of dress than emulation of the underdress of the L'Ordre du Saint-Esprit in France, which Charles would have seen during his exile while visiting the court of his cousin Louis XIV. This type of underdress lasted until the late 19th century, but in the 1840s Queen Victoria acknowledged to King Louis Philippe of France that only the mantle was obligatory.[11] In fact once men rarely had to wear breeches, the idea of wearing tights and showing the entire leg was probably deemed too archaic or risibly theatrical. Though, given the many and varied styles of military uniform that men could wear below the mantle, it was an exchange of one form of highly formalized style of clothing for another.

*54. (below) A page from a notebook of the colourist
Thomas Royle 1858–60*
*Royle was a chemist who worked for Charles
Swaisland, a leading calico printer who had works at
Crayford in Kent. Swaisland was a major supplier of
printed, striped flannels. Sporting and military motifs
were popular for men's shirtings and this page shows
samples printed with 'cyanogen' or Prussian blue. This
colour had military connotations, but was also linked
to the British royal family as one of Queen Victoria's
daughters had married the heir to the Prussian
throne in 1858.*

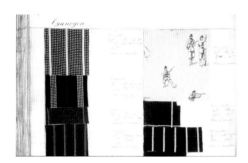

*55. (left) Lithograph of HRH The Prince of Wales, later
Edward VII c. 1865–70*
*The prince is wearing the robe of the Order of the
Garter but not the underdress introduced by Charles
II. Instead he wears a military uniform, a compromise
that blurs the notions of a chivalric but essentially
non-military order with the official dress of an officer.
Traditional forms of ceremonial dress change slowly
but this may reflect the fact that they are a form of
occasional and dignified disguise not worn often
enough to cause concern about their archaic features.*

In France the Revolution had offered an opportunity for a complete revision of ceremonial dress, and the artists David and Le Sueur produced a range of designs for official garments. The reintroduction of court ceremonial in 1804 for the coronation of Napoleon as Emperor led to lavish expenditure upon appropriate garments for both sexes. When the exhibition The Age of Napoleon was shown at the Costume Institute of the Metropolitan Museum in New York in 1989–90 it drew upon considerable work undertaken at the Musée de la Mode et du Costume of the Carnavalet over previous decades, which had culminated in an exhibition and book on the subject of ceremonial and civil uniforms in 1982–83. In fact the French fascination with the clothing of their defunct monarchies, admittedly using all the skills and products of their luxury industries and trades, has been more marked than in other countries that retain hereditary rulers. Collections and some displays of ceremonial garments can also be found in a number of European countries that had or still have monarchies, in Scandinavia, the Netherlands, Russia and the United Kingdom. The British collection has been assembled over the last 25 years and benefited at the outset from the enthusiasm of an individual collector of men's ceremonial uniforms. It now encompasses both female and male garments and, as the Royal and Ceremonial Dress Collection, is housed at Kensington Palace in London.

An element common to nearly every type of ceremonial dress is that any change to it is incremental and has only a passing acquaintance with changes in fashion. Surveying everything from academic gowns to chivalric robes offers evidence that dignity is bestowed by the historicism of the form. Once well-meaning innovators have tinkered with it, it can become absurd. One notable exception is the excellent modern embroideries on church vestments but they are adapted to the existing shape of the garment. Fashion designers can modernize the look of an airline crew or even a police force because the clothing is functional and has to work within modern conditions. Allowing a fashion designer to redesign robes worn by the wives of hereditary peers, as Norman Hartnell did for the 1953 coronation, was unfortunate. The reason for this commission was to provide appropriate robes for those who had not inherited them. Gradual adaptations had taken place to these robes since the 18th century but the change had been incremental and had retained a degree of dignified continuity. Hartnell, who designed memorable dresses for the Queen, other royal ladies and many aristocratic wives, failed dismally with his simplified design for peers' wives. It looked like a fur-trimmed, sleeveless dressing gown and was accompanied with a small fur-edged cap, both rather sub-New Look and wholly dissimilar to the existing robes. It is a salutary example of how reinterpreting the past with sensitivity is not necessarily the forte of fashion designers.

Vintage: playing with the past

Applying the word vintage to clothing is a comparatively recent phenomenon, but just like the idea of fine wine put down for future consumption, it suggests desirable items from a more brilliant past. Specialist dealers in second-hand clothing have existed for centuries; some were pawnbrokers, but all of them had purchasers from all areas in society. In earlier chapters of this book we have seen how interesting garments and textiles, new and old, were acquired by actors, artists, collectors and theatre managers of whom only a fraction actually wanted to wear the garments when adapted to suit their physiques and needs. The tradition of giving garments to poor relations or servants, cutting them up for children's clothing or making them into soft furnishing was indicative of the value placed on the fabrics. Families who kept garments because they did not need to recycle them but cherished the garments' original associations, such as weddings, court suits or dresses and coronation robes, had attics or spare rooms that later generations could raid for every sort of dressing up, from children's charades to fancy-dress balls. There was no reverence about these garments, just a sensible pragmatism, probably tinged with amusement at such curiosities. It was, however, quite rare for clothing from an earlier generation to be worn in an unaltered state because it offered an alternative construction of identity. Victorian women might play at dressing in the style of the 18th century – the dresses of the 1870s with 'Watteau' pleats from the shoulders are an example of this – but the actual dress was constructed along contemporary lines. To wear a surviving 18th-century dress for other than fancy dress would have been thought eccentric.

The rediscovery of the pleasure of wearing clothes from a previous period as everyday wear, and this is much more of a female preoccupation than a male one, really came into its own with the more-or-less coincidental development of the charity shop and the auctioning of clothes from the past in the 1960s. Imperceptibly at first there was recognition that well-made, unusual and beautiful clothing could be acquired at a fraction of the cost of couture or even High Street garments. In tandem with the exploration of the exotic (flower power), the nostalgic (Laura Ashley) and other explorations of the possibilities of individuality in dress, there was a recognition of the beauty and craft skills found in early 20th-century clothing. Paisley shawls were an acceptable acknowledgment of 19th-century technical weaving and printing of fabrics, but no one wanted to wear the clothes, as they were wholly unsuited to modern life. Fortuny was one of the early 'finds': the model Tina Chow assembled a collection of his pleated Delphos dresses and printed velvet coats and jackets in the 1970s. Once rediscovered, Fortuny's garments quickly became classics, much sought after by collectors, dealers and museums. As more was seen of and published about major 20th-century designers and those less known but talented copyists of their work, the interest in such clothing grew. By the 1990s specialist dealers and stylists were aware that they could offer clients a rare, if not unique look. Once film or television stars found the clothes irresistible, the vintage movement became big business.

The reasons why such women should choose to wear a dress by Balenciaga or Valentino, for instance, from a period of less than 40 years earlier is uncertain. It would be pleasing to believe that this might indicate an interest in the history of fashion, but it is more likely that the novelty value of the dress or perhaps a desire to identify with a semi-mythical age of Hollywood stardom are factors. It could be pure publicity – a wish to avoid the obvious contemporary designers and their identifiably stock responses to dressing the modern celebrity in keeping with their latest collections. If Givenchy's muse was Audrey Hepburn (another idea, much vaunted by designers, that they have a 'perfect woman' who wears their clothes with peerless ease), it is not difficult to imagine that a modern celebrity, but not a muse, might wish to muddle the signals and opt for the past rather than the present, if only for an important event.

Designers also delve into the past and have assistants who search for visual source material so that influences of past and present merge and are rebalanced to suit modern tastes. Vivienne Westwood's interests have been wide-ranging but a continuing delight in the fashions and forms of the 18th century can be seen in her work and she has a rare gift for using the sources with originality and wit. Designers must be showmen and women, constantly searching for novelty to create a powerful impact on the catwalk and for the watching media. The exotic nature of modern couture clothes, which often seem more like fancy dress than fashion, is the public aspect of the designers' roles as players in multinational conglomerates that sell accessories, luggage, cosmetics and scent as well as exquisitely made garments to the few women who can afford the more wearable examples of their seasonal output. The past is a quarry of ideas; John Galliano has used bias cutting, presumably knowing that it was a feature of the dresses of Vionnet and others in the 1930s. However, those who write about his work seem never to have heard of her and why should he disabuse them? Scavenging is natural for all creative artists, who can take a bit of this, a soupçon of that, and have a great deal of innate talent in understanding how colours, techniques and decoration can pay homage to the past but be wholly of the present.

Obviously the interest in and the market for vintage clothing are much wider than this high-profile world. Young women raid their mother's or grandmother's wardrobes for something that might work for them. When interviewed, as a number regularly are because vintage provides good copy for magazines, they are refreshingly honest about their attitude to the treasures that come their way. Those who speak about this are often in a business that requires heightened visual awareness, and they are aware of the likely impact of the unusual. Their reasons for recycling vary. The actress Sophie Hunter says she never buys expensive designer clothes and mixes different periods of vintage garments to suit her style: 'Some people who walk into my bedroom think it looks like a theatre dressing-room because I have everything hanging up on doors and walls'.[12] Deborah Brett, a fashion editor, does not like '...rummaging around in vintage shops and the rest of my wardrobe is a mix of current designer labels and high street pieces. But (my grandmother's) clothes are real family treasures'[13]. This contrast between nostalgic association and a sense of innate theatricality are not dissimilar to how garments would have been treated in previous centuries. Family lace or a veil might be worn for weddings across several generations, and fancy dress was inherently theatrical, even if the outfit was adapted from something old rather than specially made. What would have been thought odd was the wish to wear such clothing regularly. Today's vintage enthusiasts do not want to re-live the past or even poke gentle fun at it; they admire the fine fabrics, the craft skills and enjoy the originality such garments offer them.

Re-enactment: living the past?
If, as the novelist L P Hartley believed, 'the past is a foreign country', why would anyone wish to live in it? There are no obvious answers. By the 18th century ideas about the past were inextricably linked with the forging of national identity as Linda Colley analyzed and described in her book *Britons*. The interweaving of myth and actual events found expression on the stage, in novels, in history painting and in a delight in occasional disguise or fancy

56. Advertisement from The Graphic, *1897*
The young woman of the 1890s in her practical
cycling suit of jacket and knickerbockers, or
'Bloomers' as they were sometimes called, was a
comparatively rare sight. The majority of women who
cycled opted for a skirt or divided skirts. This may
explain the accident, as the unsuspecting man
encountered a hill and a bifurcated young woman at
the same time. By inference, if not intention, the
young woman is the more sensible of the two,
sedately wheeling her cycle downhill.

dress. However, like the vintage movement described earlier, there was no real desire to reconstruct a past and to inhabit it, using replica utensils, wearing replica clothing and adopting a persona who had a role within society in a particular historical period. Societies for re-enacting battles, groups who present movement, music and dance, interpreters in museums and historic buildings, individuals and families committed to living history are a phenomenon of the last 40 years. Those involved in re-enactment and living history enjoy using the results of their research in a wholly empirical way: spinning and weaving cloth, constructing garments, experimenting with natural dyestuffs, testing the nearest modern equivalents to the garments of their chosen period of history by regular use. The approach is not dissimilar to that of 18th- and 19th-century theatre performers in terms of their acceptance of the latest needs and research, their ownership of their own garments, and being known for the roles they inhabit within the wider repertoire of historic periods.

This interest in re-enactment is found in Great Britain, Europe and North America and has its origins in significant periods in a nation's history – the 17th-century Civil Wars in Great Britain, the American Civil War and the Napoleonic Wars in Europe – although some groups look at much earlier and later periods of conflict. As these separate groups grew in size and decided that they wanted not only to re-enact specific key events, momentous battles for example, but also to find recognition beyond their immediate circle, their wish for the nearest modern equivalent to accuracy spawned cottage industries to provide the clothes and artefacts for this alternative life. *The Living History Digest*, a British magazine with an international readership, gives details of suppliers, a comprehensive listing of all events that might be of interest to its subscribers, book reviews and reports from groups across Europe. The events diary for the period from March to October 2003 listed 192 events in Great Britain and Europe. Some events are multi-period; others are connected with a specific period in history from Roman times up to the 19th century. The suppliers can provide everything from weapons to cloth and specific items of dress, although pure wool knitted stockings are listed at prices 'from £20', a not inconsiderable sum.[14] In fact an entire outfit might easily cost £1000, far more than the owner might spend on his or her 20th-century garments.[15] One measure of the group's success is their involvement in film or television productions or regular engagement to take part in events at historic sites. It is a sophisticated business; in *The Living History Digest* nearly everyone has an email address and many have websites, but it is also an alternative reality in which the clothing and the craft skills are major elements.

Allied to re-enactment are interpreters at historic sites whose role is to introduce visitors to the customs, etiquette and clothing worn at various phases in the history of a building, including fort, palace and settlement. The research may be equally, if not more painstaking and the expenditure on the garments as costly, but this is usually a job rather than a way of life. It is a living museum of personalities and attitudes of the past rather than living within the past. The skills required to research and make the clothing – finding fabrics, investigating accurate patterns and colours – are, in both areas, highly sophisticated. Public expectation is high, fed on a diet of sleekly sanitized films, and television documentaries and dramas in which the production values in terms of costume are more demanding than in most contemporary theatre productions. However, as reality television has indicated in recent years, if individuals or families are required to live according to the hygiene and sanitary levels of previous centuries, the glamour soon fades. Denied daily baths and showers and the battery of personal toiletries, washing machines and dry cleaners that are now taken for granted, and slaving to clean houses dressed in layers of restrictive clothing, few of the participants seemed to want to live like that permanently – it is too alien to modern ideas of choice and freedom in matters of the body and the construction of personal identity.

Another aspect of this mismatch between past and present became apparent during work on an Arts & Humanities Research Board (AHRB) project in the UK in 2002. This required a group of performers to rehearse for a month in clothing as close as could be afforded to that worn by men and women in 1815. They treated it like 'costume' not clothing and were reluctant to explore its possibilities fully. They were accustomed to the idea that costume is 'directed' as much as speech and movement and found changing this view quite tricky. The young women performers were particularly shocked at the idea of wearing no drawers or the open drawers that were introduced at that time and insisted upon wearing modern panties under them. In a modern age that reveals more flesh than any other, young British women were constrained by modesty and modern taboos about what was acceptable.[16] Even children, who are often introduced to the history of dress in museums by trying on replica versions of what their Victorian ancestors might have worn, soon tire of the constraints once the novelty value, often of short duration, has faded. Living in the past or re-living it is an interesting phenomenon but denying what we know and recapturing the 'otherness' of a previous age is impossible.

57. Evening jacket c. 1930; photograph by John Chase
This silk brocade jacket has an abstract pattern of leaves overlaid with a foliage pattern in gold lamé, with Angora rabbit-fur trimming. Influenced by but inferior to the printed evening jackets of Fortuny, this is exactly the type of garment that might appeal to stylists who seek-out 'vintage' items for their clients to wear.

58. Children in replica costume

One method of assisting children to understand the way their ancestors might have lived in the past is to commission replicas of the type of clothing they could have worn. This is as popular with parents and teachers as with the children, and there is an undoubted element of 'fancy dress' about the process, but it can satisfy the need to go beyond the forbidding glass of a display to examine something of the constraints such garments imposed.

The process of making the replicas was recorded in a report compiled for Chertsey Museum in 2000. Although the museum did not have examples of everything required, the girl's chemise, drawers, bustle, dress, mantle and boots were based on surviving adult examples in the collection, and a pattern for a corset was taken from Nora Waugh's book, Corsets and Crinolines.

7 Theatrical dress: costume or fashion?

'Lacking a luxurious court to set styles, fashion turned to the theatre, with its performers and fantasies, as a source of inspiration'. S Blum[1]

Arguably the ultimate form of disguise associated with the subject of dress/fashion is theatrical costume. Despite the excellent scholarship into many aspects of theatre and performance that has been undertaken in recent years, the sheer breadth and range of the subject of costume for performance has attracted relatively little informed attention. Much more research and publication has taken place in the area of dress/fashion on film, possibly because it is perceived as a mass-cultural phenomenon rather than an elite one, but that overlooks the popular appeal of theatrical performance before the invention of film in the 1890s. Those scholars who do venture into the field are rarely dress historians. *The Clothes That Wear Us, Essays in Dressing and Transgressing in Eighteenth-Century Culture* includes a few essays on dress and performers, though the title of the collection is suggestive of the theoretical viewpoint of the editors and their contributors. However, none of the essays attempts to tackle the complex nature of the role of dress within and outside the theatre and the relevance of both to the understanding of why and how the world of the theatre offers a largely unexplored perspective on fashion and the construction of individual identity. Standard narrative histories of theatrical costume are relatively few – in the last 50 years only two of any consequence have been published, James Laver's *Costume in the Theatre* (1964) and Diana de Marly's *Costume on the Stage 1600–1940* (1982), and they merely allude to those areas that link theatrical costume to allied topics and interests with which this book is concerned.

The purpose of this chapter is to offer an introductory consideration of how and why the clothing worn for performance can afford an extra dimension to the understanding of dress in society. The dress of the theatre can be seen as a microcosm of all the other themes explored in this book: the fascination with the past and its interpretation in various publications, many of which were aimed at actors, designers and managers, and the relationship between artists and the theatre and the consequent impact on the changing styles of theatre costume. Equally important are the changing attitudes towards fashions outside and within the theatre and the impact of one on the other. The manner in which clothes were recycled and reused for stage wear was not dissimilar to that demonstrated in everyday life, and the accumulation of collections of theatre costume as records of individuals and/or significant designers complements the collecting impulses discussed elsewhere in this book.

Definitions and attitudes
Dress for performance, most usually described today as stage costume, but in the past, often called dress or habits, encompasses any and every sort of stage in the post-1660

period: barns, booths, halls throughout Europe and North America and buildings specifically designed as theatres. The physical space and conditions under which a performance took place had an impact on both performers and audience, and issues such as proximity to the performers, scenery or the lack of it, artificial or natural light, and the number of performers are elements within the presentational choices open to the performer and the responses the audience might make. In the simplest performances the lack of scenery and lighting shifted responsibility for convincing an audience to the appearance and dramatic skills of the performer.

The entry on stage costume in *The Oxford Encyclopedia of Theatre and Performance* offers the following definition: 'Distinctive clothing for individuals or groups of performers, a visual presentation of character or idea through clothed physical appearance'.[2] The idea of 'distinctive clothing' for a character or group of characters as a means of providing a visual summation of their role/s is, in one sense, not dissimilar to the impact of fashionable dress, livery or uniform on the observer. The viewer in the street or the theatre knows or thinks they know the distinctive clothing of a courtier, a soldier, a servant or a performer and will understand the roles represented by these costumes. Obviously, as with military uniforms and household liveries, there are hierarchies; the general will not look like the corporal unless the former is disguised for reasons of secrecy, again not dissimilar to strategies within a play. However, costume for performance could and often did provide an intricate set of cultural references – to nationality, gender, age, comic, tragic, antiquarian or naturalist intentions.

Stage costume in the post-1660 period could cover the spectrum of possibilities from an approximation of reality to a visual code. For example, to suggest reality a performer acting a prince or king might be clad in the actual garments borrowed from a real king in a kind of sophisticated joke between an elite group of playgoers and their favourite group of performers. The visual code made use of the elements to which more broadly based audiences had become accustomed, for example a clown's costume, which summarized the performer's comedic intentions by the recognizable shape, colours and decoration of the outfit. Before literacy was a more-or-less universal skill within western societies, costume for performance provided the visual evidence from which the audience took direct or symbolic messages about role and intention before dance, music and words added further meaning. The peripatetic nature of performers (the 'strolling player' is an apt description of the life of most performers until well into the 20th century) meant that they were seen by a great many people in many different locations and circumstances. Thus, they offered not just entertainment but a parade of clothing that ranged from the fanciful to the fashionable.

Throughout its history the theatre, however grand, however democratic its audience base, offered forms of entertainment in the disguises thought appropriate to its content at that time. The Italian designs and conventions of the High Renaissance and the Baroque, which mischievously mixed and matched contemporary styles with classical Roman tunics, metal or leather corselets, fringed leather skirts and plumed helmets for men and trailing skirts and plumed head-dresses for women, soon escaped from the elite world of fashionable artists' studios and courtly entertainments into mainstream peripatetic performance. Commedia dell'Arte characters with their distinctive costumes – notably

59. David Garrick as Richard III,
William Hogarth, 1745
*This was the role in which Garrick made his first
great success in London in 1741. In this portrait
he is wearing a quasi-historical style of costume
that hinted at a 16th-century past and remained,
with certain modifications, the stock costume for
Richard until well into the 19th century. Garrick was
the most successful actor-manager of the 18th
century and, unusually, succeeded in both tragedy
and comedy. His partnership with the painter Johann
Zoffany did much to promote theatrical portraiture
of individual performers or of scenes from a play.
Mezzotints of paintings were a useful form of
promotion and Garrick knew this, though he was
well ahead of his peers in understanding how to
use this type of publicity.*

Harlequin and Columbine – entranced audiences throughout Europe and were absorbed into different national traditions. There are many similar examples and they reflect the results of international trade and travel, and the influential engraved prints and books that recorded diverse styles of dress in all of its forms throughout the known world.

Reform of stage costume, or the lack of it, is a continuing feature of theatre history, sometimes ahead of, sometimes in tandem with, criticism of fashionable everyday clothing. In all social groups that are bound together by distinctive styles of clothing, an acceptance of the traditions and hierarchies can exist alongside a wish to subvert them. The theatre provides a number of examples of this, which offer an insight into how performers reflected contemporary trends or even led them. In the 1690s if not earlier there was a simmering feud between tragedians and comedians. A tradition that can be traced back to the classical period of Greek drama considered tragedies a superior form to comedies, although audiences might not always agree with this distinction. Colley Cibber's autobiography, published in 1740 but recalling a career that began in 1690, explained how comedians resented the money spent on costumes for tragedians, associating the investment more with 'the real than the fictitious Person of the Actor' and conversely tragedians feeling injured 'when the *Comedian* pretended to wear a fine Coat!'[3] Cibber was a successful comedian and goes on to relate details of a dispute between himself and a tragedian over expenditure over costumes. To Cibber this was a matter of festering annoyance but the brief editor's comment prefacing the extract says, '...personal

60. The Garrick Handkerchief, 1774;
photograph by John Chase
Of white calico printed in indigo, the handkerchief
displays a central motif of Garrick surrounded by
ovals containing him in five other roles, 15 other
actors (several in various roles) and two actresses. In
the four corners are the playwrights William
Shakespeare, Ben Jonson, John Fletcher and John
Dryden. There is an inscription embroidered in silk
with the words 'Susanna Pearce July the 9 1774'.
Printed handkerchiefs were popular souvenirs from
the 1750s onwards and were printed with stylized
patterns or useful information such as street maps,
but theatrical versions are rare. The central image of
Garrick as Richard III is based on the mezzotint after
Hogarth's painting (see Fig. 59). There are, in addition
to the central motif, five ovals in which he is depicted
in a mixture of comic and tragic roles. Edmund Burke
said of Garrick that '...he raised the character of his
profession to the rank of a liberal art'.

animosities among the players were kindled *even by their costumes*' [my italics]. To Nagler, the theatre historian who edited the extracts, this seemed trivial but what Cibber is suggesting is far from trivial: he is discussing the disjuncture between clothes for performance and personal clothing. He is allowing us to catch a glimpse of one of the most telling conundrums in any discussion of theatre costume: is it merely a prop, a tool for projecting a heightened reality for the consumption of a paying and potentially critical audience or is it more than that? Are the performer in character and the performer as a private individual located in a continuum, within which costume/clothing is essential to the construction of a fashioned identity that is indivisibly that of a performer who never actually escapes into a private persona? This premise might seem to be confirmed by the manner in which present-day performers, though usually in contemporary film or television roles, sometimes have a clause in their contract that allows them to acquire, at cost or sometimes as an outright gift, the 'costumes' they have briefly inhabited as gigolo, spy, gangster or heroine. Do these garments offer a tangible memory of circumstances more readily controlled in fiction if not in reality?

However, to return briefly to the costume wars between tragedians and comedians in the late 17th and early 18th centuries, Cibber supported his case with the example of the Irish comedian Thomas Doggett. Doggett was his contemporary and one-time partner as manager at Drury Lane Theatre who '…could not, with Patience, look upon the costly Trains and Plumes of Tragedy, in which knowing himself to be useless, he thought were all a vain Extravagance…'[4] This grandiose but historically suspect form of costume for female and male performers was derived from the supposedly classical Roman style mentioned earlier. The scale of the garments in both height and width dominated the stage, which was fine for declamatory speeches but impeded movement. This led, gradually, to general ridicule, which focused on the huge plumes of feathers and the heavy sweeping trains of this stylized convention to which tragic performers of both sexes held onto as a visual badge of their superiority in the theatrical pecking order. Ideas about reforming stage costume continued intermittently for the next two centuries, informed by the growing interest in antiquarian studies. Such ideas reflected a contemporary fascination with the past viewed through the prism of periods in history popularized by books and paintings and a slow but incremental distancing of stage costume from contemporary fashion. Most performers in the 18th century and into the 19th century mixed contemporary dress with costumes suggestive of character type, building up their own personal stock even when they were in companies that might provide some or all of their stage clothes. Spirited advocates for change were found in England, France and other European countries.

One early idealist was Aaron Hill, whose play *The Generous Traitor, or Aethelwold* was to be performed at Drury Lane Theatre in 1731. He argued for something approximating the type of dress worn by pre-Norman Conquest Saxons. He even supplied potential sources and some sketches to persuade the management of the theatre of the inappropriateness '…of dressing characters *so far back*, in time, after the common fashions of our days, it weakens *probability*, and cuts off, in great measure, what *most strikes* an audience …'[5] He was a realist in regard to both funding this experiment, suggesting '…giving *new* uses, to the *old* reserves of your wardrobe' and, accepting the tragedians' preference for heroic plumes, offered a compromise of coronets with one long feather each rather than the towering plumes because the former would be '…light, and may be worn, throughout five acts, without warmth or inconvenience'.[6] As the play only had two performances, it seems unlikely that a cost-conscious management would have adapted any of their existing costumes to quasi-Saxon styles, and Hill continued to criticize the costume system within the theatre. Some indication of what he found incongruous can be found in Thomas Jefferys' *A Collection of Dresses of Different Nations, Ancient and Modern, Particularly Old English Dresses. After the designs of Holbein, Vandyke, Hollar and others, with an account of the authorities from which the figures are taken, and some short historical remarks on the subject*, the first two volumes of which were published in 1757 and the last two in 1772. For everyone who could afford this series there would have been thousands more who saw some of the 480 costumes he illustrated on the stage. The volumes contain examples of stage costumes and Jefferys sensibly aimed his massive achievement at a mixed readership of artists, theatre designers and anyone seeking inspiration for masquerade costumes. The origins of the ideas discussed in chapter 1, which assumed that books on the dress of the past were mostly of use to history painters, rich patrons of masquerades or fancy dress balls and theatre designers, can be found in the mid-18th century.

61 a–g. Handkerchief details;
all photographed by John Chase
The following seven details from the handkerchief offer a brief guide to some of the stage costumes, both traditional and innovative, with which audiences at theatres and fairground acting booths would have been familiar in the second half of the 18th century.

61a. Detail depicting Garrick as Fribble in
Miss in her Teens
Garrick spent only one season at Covent Garden and wrote the farce and the role of the fop for himself in 1747. Charles Mosley made an engraving of him and his fellow performers onstage in the same year. Performers once associated with a part often played it until late in their careers.

61b. Detail depicting Garrick as King Lear
Contemporaries thought Garrick's depiction of
madness the finest they had seen but he played the
role in a contemporary dress, as he did Macbeth.

61c. Detail of Harry Woodward as Captain Bobadil in
Every Man in His Humour
Woodward was a comedian in Garrick's Drury Lane
Company and Bobadil was a role in which he
excelled. He also wrote pantomimes and was an
acclaimed Harlequin. The swaggering quasi-
17th-century style of costume was retained
within the traditions of burletta and melodrama
into the 19th century.

Theatrical dress: costume or fashion?

Commentators both within and outside the theatre focused upon the incongruities of stage costume: its variability in quality, its inappropriateness, its historical inaccuracies. A particular complaint involved the topsy-turvy world in which leading performers acting the parts of servants wore finer clothing than minor performers who, in the play, were in roles of their social superiors. This is suggestive of similar comments and veiled criticisms made by foreign visitors who were startled when, in the everyday world, they saw maids dressed almost as finely as their employers and gentlemen in the casual garb of countrymen, the frock coat. Whether the stage was aping reality or suggestively undermining it is unclear. However when innovations were attempted they invariably caused comment. The following few examples can be extended by reading Diana de Marly's *Theatre Costume* 1600–1940. However a certain caution should be exercised about her views that the stage invariably followed the fine arts and conformist ideas of social etiquette, missing the point that theatre, and its performers, are often intentionally subversive of the natural order.

The Irish actor Charles Macklin, a contemporary of David Garrick's, dressed both Shylock and Macbeth in new ways. In his changes, the former was seen not as a comic character (a strange idea today, but current then) but dressed in melancholic black gabardine with the red cap that Jews were forced to wear in Venice in the 18th century. Macbeth was clothed in 'the old Caledonian habit' not in the scarlet suit edged with gold braid of a contemporary English general, which was Garrick's preferred costume for the role.[7] John Philip Kemble discarded the quasi-17th-century Vandyke costume for Hamlet when he made his London debut in the role in 1783, preferring '...a modern court dress of rich black velvet, with a star on the breast, the garter and pendant ribband of an order'. Later in his career he did wear what de Marly calls Vandyke dress but is actually closer to a medieval tunic and cloak.[8] If stage costume is heightened reality, a means by which a performer distinguishes character type before the audience responds to words, gesture and plot, it seems probable that Kemble intentionally based his discontented Danish prince on another prince – the current Prince of Wales, later Prince Regent and George IV, who at the time of Kemble's performance was already notorious for his disagreements with his father and his liaison with an actress. Kemble, like all of his talented siblings, four of whom (John Philip, his sister Sarah Siddons, his brothers Stephen and Charles) entered their parents' profession, was interested in the arts, literature and history and was socially adept. Both John Philip and Charles combined a flair for innovation with a shrewd ability to use their fame and influence to shift audience perceptions in line with new ideas about how to present plays, most notably in regard to scenery and costumes.

J P Kemble popularized the use of the toga for roles such as Julius Caesar and Coriolanus, aware of François-Joseph Talma's innovations in France; Lawrence's monumental portraits of Kemble suggest a man born to portray neoclassicism on the stage but, like all intelligent and powerful actor–managers, he was keeping abreast of new ideas and trends, a protagonist for a type of neoclassicism that symbolized ideas of change well beyond the theatre. His younger brother Charles enlisted J R Planché, that polymath figure we encountered in chapter 1, to design costumes in the early 1820s for *King John* and *Henry IV*, which translated to the stage the gothic medievalism that Walter Scott's novels had made so fashionable. These changes were beginning to fulfil a prophetic view propounded by John Hill in his treatise *The Actor*, written as far back as 1750. Among his many tips and strictures he wrote that, '...the habits of characters on the stage should be proper as well as pretty; and that the actors are not only to dress so as not to offend probability, but they are to be ty'd down as much as painters to the general customs of the world. Alexander the great, or Julius Caesar, wou'd appear as monstrous to us in bag wigs on the stage as in a picture ...'.[9] The comparison with painting is pressed further in the same treatise: 'He cannot too frequently remember that the representation of a play is a sort of painting, which owes all its beauty to a close imitation of nature, and that its touches are expected to be even vastly more expressive than those of the pencil[10]...'. Closely imitating nature in this context would have meant aiming for the type of accuracy found in history painting and been made possible by the growing body of information on the dress and furnishings of the past. The Kembles applied this advice, and the pursuit of the archaeologically and pictorially correct can be traced from them through the careers of other powerful actor–managers such as William Macready, Charles Kean and Henry Irving until it expired with the excesses of Herbert Beerbohm Tree, although not before inspiring Cecil B de Mille and influencing the costumes found in historical epics of the cinema. Charles Kemble took his company to France in the late 1820s where they made a huge impact on artists, musicians and writers. But Macready and Irving were shrewd enough to recognize a much bigger, English-speaking, audience in North America where their approach to stage costume, scenery and performing style made a considerable impression on American practices.

This epic style of historically accurate performance was increasingly popular with bourgeois families throughout Europe and America. It was not raffish: texts were often bowdlerized, scenes inserted to enhance the text, action often frozen for a few seconds to allow the audience to imagine a painting within the proscenium arch, to produce a carefully sanitized, exquisitely dressed past fabricated to meet the educational expectations of new audiences. It was, or so it seemed, 'living history', closer to the re-enactment movement today than an intellectual understanding of how costume might impede understanding by overwhelming the text with overly researched set-piece historicism. The costumes were often designed or supervised by leading artists, the music composed by distinguished musicians and verse dramas written by leading poets. It was educational and visually spectacular and attracted new audiences to the theatre. Fortunately, alongside this high-minded respectability there existed a joyously subversive set of performing traditions, such as melodrama, burletta and music hall. The popularity of all forms of theatre and the diverse backgrounds of its performers allowed ideas on art, design and literature to be absorbed or discarded, as seemed applicable to the circumstances. Amateur theatricals, an increasingly popular activity in the 19th century, allowed intrigued middle-class amateurs to begin performing or, in certain instances, decide to become professionals. The growing taste for the elegant comedies of Pinero and Wilde offered new opportunities to aspirant performers from many social backgrounds. Performers to whom the social etiquette of the world portrayed on the stage and the clothes worn were inbred gradually took roles in such plays. Performing the 'self' gradually took over from performing the 'other' (when a performer imagined and

61d. *Detail of Samuel Foote as Mother Cole in* The Minor
Foote was an actor–manager and dramatist who took over the Haymarket Theatre in 1747. He played comic roles and wrote his best play The Minor *in 1760. He disliked Garrick and lampooned him mercilessly. Here he is 'cross-dressed' wearing the type of outfit for old women also worn by male performers for the witches in Macbeth.*

61e. *Detail of Thomas Weston as Dr Last in* The Devil on Two Sticks
Weston was a comedian who, like many other performers, had spent time acting in fairground booths. He worked with Foote at the Haymarket and for Garrick at Drury Lane.

61f. Detail of Charles Macklin as Shylock in The Merchant of Venice
Macklin rescued Shylock from the low comedy part it had become since the Restoration. He first played the part at Drury Lane in 1741 and was immediately acclaimed for both his interpretation and the type of costume he chose: a long black gabardine coat and a scarlet hat, the dress of Venetian Jews. Zoffany painted him in the role c. 1768 and there are two engravings of 1769.

61g. Detail of Mrs Yates (Mary Ann Graham) as Mandane in Cyrus
One of the finest tragic actresses of the 18th century, Mrs Yates was a member of Garrick's Drury Lane Company from 1754. Here she is seen in the typical tragedienne's costume of wide skirts and long train, with a quasi-oriental headdress, hanging sleeves and overskirt faintly suggestive of a Turkish or Persian gown. The printer seems to have muddled his engravings of Mrs Yates. The role of Mandane was one of her most acclaimed, but the play was The Orphan of China, *an adaptation of Voltaire's* L'Orphelin de la Chine.

interpreted a social role with which they are unfamiliar). However, movements in realist or constructivist drama in the late 19th and early 20th centuries maintained the illusion of a separate world in which the performers' words, gestures and costumes were constructed to create alternative realities. This diversity of theatrical forms was gradually matched and overtaken by film. The early silent films offered their audience 'moving pictures', which built on observation learned in and from the theatre; emotions, gestures and costume presented more information than the music and sub-titles. Reading the visual imagery, however nuanced or crude, eventually found expression in Roland Barthes' essay, 'The Romans in Films'. He considered the costumes and hairstyles seen in the 1953 version of *Julius Caesar* and was particularly fascinated by the visual symmetry of the men's hairstyles. In fact what Hollywood perceived of as a 'Roman' style had its theatrical origins in pre-1800 France and the friendship between the painter David and the actor Talma.

Performers, audiences and clothes

Although performance had not wholly disappeared during the Commonwealth period (1649–1660), the reintroduction of licensed theatres in the United Kingdom was due to Charles II's enthusiasm for plays. The two new theatres catered for a fairly wide range of the capital's population, with the shortfall easily met by the many fairs in London and the regions. The principal innovation that is associated with Restoration theatre is the female performer. The stage offered women a means, admittedly in some instances financially and socially insecure, of earning a living, including writing for the stage, as Aphra Behn and others did from the 1670s onwards. What tends to exercise the minds of scholars today are the 'breeches roles' that predated Mrs Bloomer's experiment by approximately 200 years. The perception of this transgressive clothing as either empowering or exploiting needs to be placed in the context of the experimentation by elite women throughout the 17th century with masculine doublets, riding-habits and hats. What the stage presented was the natural conclusion of this elite playfulness, a form of disguise that caused uncertainty as well as titillation. Pepys, unsurprisingly, admired Nell Gwynn, actress and mistress to Charles II whom he saw on several occasions as Florimel in Dryden's *Secret Love or the Mayden Queen* in 1667. She appeared as '...a mad girle and then, most and best of all, when she comes in like a young gallant; and hath the motions and carriage of a spark, the most that ever I saw any man have'.[11] She seems to have been preferable to Mary Davis, another of Charles II's mistresses, who did not convince Pepys when he saw her 'dance in boy's clothes'.[12] The actress Mrs Anne Bracegirdle (c.1663–1748) excelled in comedy, '...and that too when in Men's Cloaths, in which she far surmounted all the Actresses of that and this Age. – Yet, she had a Defect scarce perceptible, viz., her right Shoulder a little protended, which, when in Men's Cloaths, was cover'd by a long or Campaign Peruke. – She was finely shap'd, and had very handsome Legs and Feet; and her Gait, or Walk, was free, manlike, and modest, when in Breeches'.[13] It is possible that Anne Bracegirdle, a celebrated Millamant in *The Way of the World*, found masculine disguise offered her a wider range of roles and greater opportunities of expression if she ignored gender stereotyping.

Many actresses specialized in such roles or played them within a much wider range of parts. It is likely that a theatrical background, with its emphasis on role-playing and transformation, removed barriers found elsewhere in society. Charlotte Charke (1713–60) was the youngest child of Colley Cibber and in her youth much preferred masculine to feminine pursuits, often dressing as a boy to hunt, ride and shoot. She had two brief marriages and tried a number of theatrical and non-theatrical careers; the latter included working as a valet and a waiter. As an actress she performed at licensed theatres, in fairground acting booths and toured provincial theatres. She acted in both male and female parts and adopted the persona and clothing of 'Mr Brown' when she toured the provinces.[14] She had such a successful season in 'breeches roles' in 1744 that she was able to live on the profits until 1746.[15] Some actresses were reluctant about such roles and found compromise costumes. Sarah Siddons seemed, within the great Kemble family of actors, to have been more conservative than her famous siblings, John Philip and Charles, both of whom were innovators. However she was still prepared to play Hamlet, as did the American actress Charlotte Cushman later in the 19th century, and, most notably Sarah Bernhardt, also in the 19th century. In the early 19th century, Jane Scott, who as playwright, theatre-manager and leading actress was wholly beyond any pressure to perform any parts she did not prefer, kept the tradition alive in burletta. One such role was that of a dashing junior naval officer in *The Inscription* in 1815. Her more celebrated younger contemporary Madame Vestris (1797–1856) was unrivalled in male roles. She played the hero in *Giovanni in London*, a burlesque on the Mozart opera in 1820, and first appeared at Covent Garden in 1821 as Macheath in *The Beggar's Opera*. She too was a theatre manager, and appeared in J R Planché's extravaganzas written for Covent Garden. These were prototype principal boy roles in entertainments such as *Puss in Boots*, which she performed from 1837 onwards.[16]

Fanny Kemble (1809–93), the actress daughter of Charles Kemble, settled in America as the wife of Pierce Butler and startled her circle of new friends by adopting male garments. In 1838 it was noticed that, 'Mrs Butler arrays herself in her riding costume – white pants (tout à fait à la mode des messieurs) and habit, with a black velvet jacket and cap, very picturesque'.[17] Five years later another American, Mrs Charles Ingersoll, wrote to Fenimore Cooper that, 'It seems Mrs Butler is a good fisherman, and she made a great deal of cancan by wearing pantaloons, with boots and straps, a man's hat with blouse overall. She rode miles on horseback alone, in petticoats, and fished in pantaloons, which Charles said, was unreasonable, if not in bad taste'.[18] Quite what we are to make of this is open to debate. Was Fanny Kemble an inveterate performer, even in private life, or was she eminently practical? Certainly she predated Mrs Bloomer, though not Georges Sand, the celebrated and strong-willed French novelist, who often wore male garments for comfort and anonymity.

Some, though not all, actresses experimented with clothing both on and off the stage; a notable example is Ellen Terry (1847–1938). She came from a theatrical family and started her career as the boy Mamillius in Charles Kean's production of *The Winter's Tale*. She was a convincing Viola in *Twelfth Night* in 1884–5 wearing white hose and a knee-length white tunic embroidered with gold thread, a short cloak, ruff and cap, and regretted not playing Rosalind in *As You Like It*.[19] She was closely linked with the world of the arts; her public life as a performer and her private life had been indelibly marked by her first and short-lived marriage to the painter G F Watts and her liaison with E W Godwin. She took considerable and informed interest in her own costumes and, both on and off-stage, was associated with the aesthetic dress movement. Her boyish elegance – she was tall and slender – and fluid movements allowed her to create roles that set fashions.[20] The impact that she made in the 18th-century costumes for *Olivia* in 1878, designed by the artist Marcus Stone, was recollected by a playwright colleague: 'It touched the fashions. It left its record in "The Queen", and all the modes were influenced by the sweet parson's daughter. Olivia's cap was everywhere ...'.[21] As Marguerite in *Faust* she was copied in the opera house and at fancy dress parties. In *Madame Sans Gêne* with costumes by Doucet, the fashionable French couturier, she popularized the high-waisted, Directoire-type evening dresses of the 1890s.[22] She was aware of her power as a trendsetter, delighting in her memoirs in introducing a style based upon a late-17th-century doeskin coat in the collection of the painter J A Seymour Lucas. In this instance her recollection was faulty; in fact Seymour Lucas had used this surviving man's coat as inspiration for one of Irving's costumes for *Ravenswood*.[23]

When successful actresses, like Terry, travelled between America and Europe, they were fêted, interviewed, drawn and photographed and their stage costumes and personal clothes admired and copied. Couturiers recognized the power of leading ladies of the theatre and opera, and the quotation at the beginning of this chapter, which appeared in a book of fashion plates from *Harper's Bazar* – 'Lacking a luxurious court to set styles, fashion turned to the theatre, with its performers and fantasies, as a source of inspiration' – is equally applicable outside of post-Second Empire France in the late 19th century. Terry, Mrs Patrick Campbell, Lillie Langtry and many others were featured in newspapers and magazines that recorded new productions in copious detail. In 1895 the women's pages of *The Sketch* devoted several pages to *King Arthur* at the Lyceum and though Terry's costumes were admired, Lena Ashwell in Elaine's '...simple robe of soft white silk, which might for all the world be one of Liberty's latest productions, and which is pretty enough to be copied by any modern maiden with a taste for artistic dress...', obviously entranced the journalist with its contemporary resonance.[24] Other actresses might be fashionable in a more mainstream way, such as Lillie Langtry (1853–1929), who was dressed by Worth for her role in *The Degenerates* seen in London in 1899 and New York in 1900.[25]

This fruitful interchange between performers, artists, audience and fashion was as pertinent for male performers. Cross-dressing, for instance, was not just a matter of women playing roles for which they adopted a male disguise. Male performers undertook roles in female costume for comedic or sinister effect as they had done for centuries. Traditionally the witches in *Macbeth* were played by men as comic harridans; Garrick dressed them in '...mittens, plaited caps, laced aprons, red stomachers, ruffs, &...' but J P Kemble in 1794 decided they should (though still men) be 'preternatural beings'.[26] This may not have been a successful innovation, for in an engraving of Kemble, as *Macbeth*, confronting the witches, the latter are undoubtedly comic harridans. Nearly 40 years later in 1833 Fanny Kemble, John Philip's niece, was playing in Macbeth in New York and was dismayed by '...three jolly-faced fellows with as due a proportion of petticoats as any woman, letting alone a witch, might desire, jocose red faces, peaked hats and broomsticks'.[27] She wanted 'the first melodramatic actors on the stage ... and such dresses

EDWIN BOOTH AS OTHELLO—THE CHARACTER OF THE MOOR WAS
ONE OF THE MOST REMARKABLE RÔLES IN THE GREAT
AMERICAN ACTOR'S REPERTORY

*62. (above) Edwin Booth in Othello, magazine
plate (?),1881*

*The Great American actor Edwin Booth was an
acclaimed Othello. He played a season with Henry
Irving's company at the Lyceum in 1881 during which
the actors alternated the roles of Othello and Iago.
The production was designed in a late-16th-century
style. Irving's costumes for Othello were principally in
yellows and golds and the style and colour of Booth's
gown would have complemented these. Irving used
the costumiers Madame Auguste, Monsieur Alias and
Mrs Reid; the first and last suppliers were associated
with Irving's company for much of his tenure of the
Lyceum and would have been familiar with his
production values.*

*63. (left) Suit of coat, waistcoat and breeches,
English c. 1780–85. Satin with embroidery on the
coat and waistcoat of floral motifs in coloured
silks with glass beads, seed pearls and sequins.
Photograph by John Chase.*

*Eighteenth-century suits were acquired by actors in the
nineteenth century and used for stage roles. Three that
belonged to Samuel Phelps survive; one of c. 1780 is a
formal suit with an additional and later application of
broad gold braid to make it more distinctive under
stage lighting. The size of this suit – its original owner
was tall and sturdily built – may have ensured that it
was not used for fancy dress or acquired by an actor or
artist in the nineteenth century.*

as would accord a little better with the blasted heath, the dark fungus-grown wood, the desolate, misty hill-side and the flickering light of the cauldron cave'.[28] The long-standing theatrical tradition of this style of costume for the witches can be traced back to the Irish comedian Thomas Doggett, if not earlier. His career encompassed the grandeur of the licensed theatre and the fairground acting booths of popular performance. When he appeared at Bartholomew Fair in 1701 in one comic piece he was dressed 'in old woman's petticoats and red waistcoat'.[29] Male comedians often specialized in roles that allowed them to ridicule a series of stereotypical, usually elderly women, partly because female performers preferred not to be cast in such limited and unflattering parts. However, the tradition found in *Macbeth*, of a recognizable style of costume for the cross-dressed man continued in burletta, pantomime, comic plays such as *Charley's Aunt*, and is still found today, albeit in a more realistic form, on TV and in films (*Tootsie* and *Mrs Doubtfire* are part of this long tradition).

Quite as much time and thought was expended on contemporary or near contemporary forms of costume for male performers playing male roles. Charles Mathews, the second husband of Madame Vestris, was a well-known actor in modern dress comedies. In his memoirs he claimed responsibility for introducing more subtlety into his costumes in the 1840s and 1850s:

'A claret-coloured coat, salmon-coloured trowsers with a broad black stripe, a sky-blue neckcloth with a large paste brooch, and a cut-steel eye-glass with a pink ribbon no longer marked the "light comedy gentleman" and the public at once recognised and appreciated the change.'[30]

Such broad 'caricature' costumes might identify a type of character but Mathews and other contemporaries wanted something more realistic. At much the same time that Mathews was instituting changes, both the actor–manager William Macready and the playwright Edward Bulwer Lytton were preparing the 1840 production of Lytton's new comedy *Money*. Macready, firing questions in a letter to Lytton, says of one actor, 'He also proposes a white coat and light blue trowser for his first dress – but *I do not see that.* – I like your sketch of the dresses very much ...'.[31] Lytton replied two days later: 'With regard to Smooth's white coat (I suppose great-coat), there is one objection. It is the London Season that is Summer – & besides it is a very dangerous article of dress unless the figure carries it off well. If he likes to wear it, Jackson must make it – in the present fashion – no buttons behind'.[32] Lytton was a fashionable novelist in addition to being a playwright and moved in the world portrayed in his play, and Macready was notoriously fussy about costumes, whether historic or modern. Nearly 50 years later painstaking research taken for granted. W S Gilbert not only wrote the Savoy operas with Sullivan but he also directed them and supervised the sets and costumes. When preparing *Ruddigore*, his satire about popular melodrama in 1887, he decided that the chorus of Bucks and Blades should wear early-19th-century uniforms of 20 different regiments. He was such a perfectionist that he had them checked for accuracy by the Quartermaster of the Army.[33] At the other extreme, some actors were so fashionable that their clothes were copied as templates for elegant masculinity. Sir George Alexander (1858–1918) was the most successful actor–manager in London from 1890 until his death. He played in Wilde comedies and romantic dramas and when he appeared in Pinero's *His House in Order* in 1906 wearing soft collars and lounge suits, this set an imprimatur on this less formal style of day dress for men.[34]

Audiences relished novelty and playbills, of which the earliest surviving example dates back to 1672, mentioned if there were new costumes, obviously as a major selling point. As well as being the performer's stock-in-trade, costumes were, until well into the 18th century, more significant than scenery, most especially outside major cities with permanent theatres. Given that many performers were always hoping for the opportunity to join a major company they invested as much money as they could in appropriate costumes and, quite literally, could not perform if something happened to their costumes, whether delayed in baggage carts, lost or stolen. However, it is misleading to suggest, as some modern theatre historians have done, that outside of courtly entertainments it was more usual for performers to wear costumes akin to those worn by audiences to establish a closer rapport. Foreign and exotic styles such as Spanish, French, Turkish and so-called

64. The Church Scene from Much Ado About Nothing; photograph of Johnston Forbes-Robertson's painting, 1883
Irving played Benedict (centre right) and Ellen Terry played Beatrice (third left) in a production first staged at the Lyceum in 1882. Forbes-Robertson had trained as an artist before he became an actor, and the original painting belongs to The Players Club in New York. This scene captures the overly researched historicism that was so admired by actors, their artistic advisers and audiences in the 19th century. It looks like an historical painting and was intended to instruct the audience as well as offering entertainment. Accuracy was subdued by a degree of Victorian rectitude: the women do not wear the correct stays and hoops, the men's costumes do not have codpieces and the style is an aesthetically pleasing version of the 16th century.

Theatrical dress: costume or fashion? □

Roman (meaning the classical variety) were familiar to audiences. A perennial favourite at fairs was *The Siege of Troy*, first introduced at Bartholomew Fair in 1707 by Mrs Mynns's troupe of players. A show cloth for this can be seen in Hogarth's painting and engraving of Southwark Fair (1733 and 1735 respectively). A revival of 1747 advertised that the production was '...finish'd according to the Taste of the Antient Greeks', and Skelt's juvenile play sheets of the 1820s provide evidence of the gloriously muddled mixture of classical and oriental costumes.[35] All of this could be inordinately costly but costumes were a crucial element in both attracting audiences and maintaining careers. Advertising 'new dresses' or 'new habits' on playbills was supplemented by actual display. The acting booths at fairs usually had a gallery or balcony on which the performers appeared, prior to the performance itself. In the late 1750s the comedian Thomas Weston, who later worked at Drury Lane, '...shew'd himself between every performance to the mob in his stage dress, in a gallery erected before the booth'.[36] The blend of fare was a mixture of traditional British features with novelties found at court or in licensed theatres and imported from France and Italy. Crowds then as now relished spectacle, topicality, a mix of comic and tragic with something exotic and unusual. It was not just in licensed theatres that audiences could view quasi-classical grandeur, Indian, Persian and Turkish styles; they were offered to the wider audience of the fairs and became part of the visual currency.

If a performer lost his costumes it was both a financial and business loss. In 1741 the younger Thomas Yeates had his booth burgled at Southwark Fair and lost costumes that he valued at £40, a huge sum, which effectively prevented him from performing.[37] A constant theme in the memoirs and biographies of performers – of which there are so many that the number alone indicates the importance of the theatre and its performers from the early 18th century onwards – is the cost of their clothes, the irritation with managements that offered them inappropriate costumes, and their wish, should they achieve prominence usually as actor–managers, to ensure the coherence of productions and the role of performers within them. All costume, whether traditional (deriving its impact from the familiar visual summary of stock characters) or innovative (drawing upon new ideas in antiquarian studies or research, like Godwin's, which was intensely narrow in its sense of what was true to text and historical accuracy in performance), cost money and the performer often had to provide it. The newcomer rummaged around in specialist shops, known to both actors and artists, trying to assemble the basics. Samuel Phelps (1804–78) became an actor on the York circuit in 1826 and bought 'a handful of valuable things, including a ringlet wig' from a fellow actor for a crown and then went off to purchase from a dealer '...a pair of russet boots, a pair of sandals, a pair of fleshings, a pair of worsted tights, an old sword, and a few other odds and ends, for thirty shillings'. And this was at a time when few performers earned much more than 25 shillings a week in the provinces.[38] Later, when he reached London to play supporting roles for William Macready at Covent Garden in 1837 he invested £150 in costumes, some of which were original 18th-century suits.[39] Sir John Martin-Harvey (1863–1944) made a similar visit to a dealer over 50 years later and bought red wool tights, black velveteen shoes, a sword hanger, a frock coat 'of uncertain period', and several 'black American cloth "tops" '– the last transformed a pair of black boots into a variety of styles and periods.[40]

This ingenuity was a feature of all performers' lives and their attitude towards clothing was pragmatic, as it had to be flexible and capable of as many transformations as they undertook during an engagement. If an actor died without disposing of his costumes they might be auctioned, as happened with Walter Montgomery's in 1872. Costumiers, dealers and other performers attended the sale and the 15 or so lots ranged from costumes for Shakespearean roles to more modern historical plays. The costume for Hamlet fetched 25 shillings and that for Julius Caesar 60 shillings. The report in *The Era* noted that the whole sale realized about £80 and that, 'The best prices were secured for a number of pairs of worsted and silk tights.'[41] Tights, of course, could be washed and used without adaptation, whereas costumes would need more work.

It was equally costly for women. Marie Wilton came from a theatrical family but in her memoirs she mentions her concern at getting the part of Perdita in an extravaganza based on *The Winter's Tale* in 1856 and being told to provide her own dress. Her mother made something 'out of material I have by me', a dress of white cashmere with roses at the waist.[42] Constance Benson recalled her youthful experiences in the early 1880s, when after accepting a provincial engagement for boys and second old women she was told that she had '...to provide my own dresses at a salary of a guinea a week'.[43]

Dressmaking was a useful extra skill for female performers and John Martin-Harvey's wife Nina de Silva was a skilful dressmaker when she was not acting. She joined her husband in the research into 'historical costume', which was so characteristic of that period, hunted for materials, bought whatever 'old costumes as fell within the scope of our purse', and adapted them, as required.[44] Miss de Silva was the 'deserving young actress' to whom a bequest of the wardrobe of Princess Murat was given: two huge baskets containing 'elaborate silk fronts for costumes which had never been worn, embroidered with pearls and exquisitely coloured designs, costly furs and velvet coats...'.[45] This willingness to re-use, adapt and redesign clothing from a variety of sources was also a feature of theatrical costumiers who, from the 1790s onwards, often created whole or part productions alongside large wardrobe departments in established theatres, a tradition that continues up to the present day.

65. Woman's bodice or jacket, French c. 1890-95; photograph by John Chase.
This bodice is an interesting hybrid. It has the label of 'Doucet Paris' but is remade from a man's court evening waistcoat of the 1840s or 1850s. The sturdy embroidered silk of the waistcoat has survived much better than the cream silk sleeves and back of the jacket. The finishing processes used on late 19th- and early 20th-century lightweight silks are destructive to the fabric. Doucet had an international clientele that included actresses, including Ellen Terry, for whom he provided the Directoire-influenced costumes for Madam Sans Gêne in 1897, but whether this jacket was for fancy dress, the theatre or everyday wear is impossible to determine. However, as an example of fashionable scavenging and reinvention it is ingenious and witty.

Theatrical collections

Alongside the eminently businesslike and practical approach to costume as a working tool ran a degree of sentimentality. Great performers generated mementos: costumes and properties used by them, paintings, books, working scripts and items they had acquired from an earlier generation of performers. There were also souvenirs for wider public consumption: playbills, engravings, photographs, programmes and juvenile play sheets, burnished their image and that of their profession. Obviously major libraries and museums throughout Europe and America have significant documentary and illustrative material, which are complemented by other types of collection held elsewhere. Individuals and groups assembled notable items, some of which found their way into the possession of clubs. The Garrick Club in London, established in 1831, owns an extensive collection of paintings, books and other souvenirs of distinguished performers. Following this example the Players Club in New York was set up in 1888 in a house purchased for it by Edwin Booth, its first President. It has considerable collections, which include costumes. Important collections of costume are found in many museums, some dedicated only to the theatre, others more broadly based. Archival and three-dimensional collections are attached to theatres and opera houses. This diffusion of material means that like other specialist collections mentioned in the previous two chapters the interchanges between dress/fashion and theatrical costume are rarely explored together. It is commonplace to find that writers assume that theatre costume follows contemporary fashion or, at best, exaggerates it for stage effects. In certain instances this is so, but there are exceptions, and the fact that the provenance of theatrical costumes is usually firm, and there is so much supplementary evidence to contextualize its production and use, provides considerable scope for new work looking at the connections between performance and fashion.

Conclusion

'A university culture where the appreciation of Victorian women's underwear replaces the appreciation of Charles Dickens and Robert Browning sounds like the outrageousness of a new Nathaniel West, but is merely the norm. The poems of our climate have been replaced by the body-stockings of our culture'. Professor Harold Bloom[1]

The quotations that head each chapter are intended to indicate that studying dress and fashion has always been an area of controversy. This is an excellent sign: no subject dies if it is a constant source of debate. However, what it has often lacked is a sense of proportion. In all honesty, both the construction of fashion across the ages and its consumption are innately frivolous. Obviously all sorts of processes, manufactures and trades were developed in order to clothe people, but as experiments in China during and in the aftermath of the cultural revolution demonstrated, it is possible to devise and enforce a monotone uniformity. This asexual simplicity was spotted, reinterpreted and re-coloured for western consumers, a type of hybridization found often in the history of fashion and increasingly apparent in an age when visual information wings its way around the globe so swiftly. This example could have been used in the chapter on uniformity and disguise but it fits more readily in a conclusion that has to consider humour, or the lack of it. The history of dress/fashion is full of amusement; it could be written as a satire on the credulity of consumers, in the manner of a Restoration comedy, a number of which did use fashion as a metaphor for inanity. However, the long struggle to make the subject respectable gradually omitted the humour and concentrated on the serious business of understanding, interpreting and theorizing. It is the theoreticians, more than any others who write about dress, who seem to have taken the whole subject far too seriously and, in doing so, outraged traditionalists from many disciplines. In the opening quote, the words of Harold Bloom, an unreconstructed literary scholar of the old school, could be construed as apoplectic rage or delicious irony. Having read more than one humour-free article on Victorian underclothing written by academics I can see the problem, but I do not assume that this is more than a temporary cul-de-sac. No sane person, academic or otherwise, will spend a career discussing 19th-century underclothing.

Might Harold Bloom have felt more comfortable if the Victorian underclothing had belonged to Charles Dickens and had formed only one element within a biography of him? Dickens was a dandy in his youth and biographers frequently discuss the appearance, fashionable or otherwise, of their subjects. It is unfortunate that the history of dress, though littered with intriguing and often influential wearers and makers of clothing and its many accessories, does not lend itself to biography. Just writing the history of the suit, for example, covers many centuries and, although, like a person, it is born, grows to maturity and then declines into old age, it is still with us. Its biography is open-ended, as are the biographies of many items of clothing. The purpose of this book was to introduce some of the many ways in which dress and fashion have been studied from the second half of the 17th century up to the present day. It has no agreed biographies, which is why it seems to offer successive generations of students the opportunity to reinterpret it according to the intellectual preoccupations of their period. The word biography was not chosen lightly: a biography is about a person, and the outward appearance of a person is an essential element in how they present themselves to the world. Each of us constructs an identity or identities and how we choose to do so is, in part, signified to the world by our appearance. In western countries this is, to a greater or lesser extent, dependent upon the clothing we use to cover our bodies.

We have seen how antiquarians, artists, collectors, curators, theatrical designers, journalists, early theoreticians and reformers have used and reinterpreted the evidence and information available to them. Collectors and collections that emphasized the need to understand construction and context, and demonstrated that textiles made into clothing were as important as flat textiles, replaced the early hierarchies within the subject. The multiplicity of direct and subliminal forms of information on appearance that became available during the course of the 20th century led the study of dress out of the costume museum, the economic archives and the practical needs of designers for theatre and film, into universities and many different disciplines. Dress historians had always worked within different environments so it is unsurprising that the lack of an overarching theoretical basis for the subject was spotted and explored by academics familiar with new ideas and keen to apply them within areas that seemed hopelessly out of touch. However, as the subject moved away, and repositioned itself within theoretical analysis, its academic practitioners seemed not to be interested in the contributions that collections might offer such work. Initially there was a danger that academic perceptions were limited by narrow and outdated ideas of what traditional dress historians actually did and wrote about. This lack of understanding of the complex and diverse history of the subject and an unwillingness to accept that its different approaches are valid seemed to indicate that the subject would be broken up into unconnected fragments.

It was particularly unfortunate that the growing strength of academic work was happening at much the same time as the status of collections of dress in museums was being threatened. There are still considerable problems but gradually interests are beginning to merge. A number of curators and museums are collaborating with academics to re-emphasize the importance of material culture. This is essential, as collections of dress, even comparatively recent dress, are fragile and cannot last indefinitely. They may be unrepresentative mementos of an elite culture, but within them is evidence that deserves more study than it has yet received. One garment can yield information about fabric, its use, its decoration with embroidery, braid and other techniques, all of which relate to specific crafts and skills. Its construction offers information about tailoring and dressmaking methods, which can be related to manuals, magazines and individual requirements. It forms an important element in the discussion of production processes and consumption. If it has been altered or remade it is indicative of a pragmatic re-use of clothing that is being rediscovered by those who wear the dress of the past because it has inherent beauty. It may lack animation, but its three-dimensional possibilities and the intricate connections that it provides to many artistic and social preoccupations across several centuries, are suggestive of much more than 'a fragment, a partial snapshot of dress'.

Whether dress/fashion is an art or a craft is not important. It offers a tangible expression of individuality – to anonymity, to social status, to disguise, to occupation or any combination of these possibilities. We cannot interview the majority of wearers of the dress of the past and we certainly should not attempt to imbue them with our values. We may find their attitudes and ideas alien, patriarchal or narrowly drawn, but to reconstruct their lives and the way they chose to dress in line with modern preoccupations with gender, otherness or transgression, to mention just a few modern concepts, is as short-sighted as believing that studying dress is only important as a tool for dating paintings. Understanding fashion history cannot and should not relate to modern ideas alone. The history of ideas is littered with as many honourable failures as any subject area. Unblinkered curiosity is the best attitude to bring to the study of any subject, and a useful method of harnessing curiosity is to reconsider what has gone before and not merely accept what is happening now.

In the introduction I suggested that by disentangling some of the many strands that comprise the study of dress and fashion it might be possible to discover if traditional dress history and the new dress history are compatible or destined to co-exist uneasily. There are obvious imbalances: there are more academics than curators; the former are required to undertake research and publish, the latter are not and their work is immensely time-consuming. Curators work in organizations that require teamwork and place the needs of the organization over individual achievement, and it is this that may, ultimately, prove problematic. If academics decide that collections and exhibitions offer the next interesting opportunity the curator might be pushed into a supporting role, not dissimilar to that of a wardrobe keeper in a theatre – fetching, carrying, making suggestions – but at the end of the day more akin to a junior than an equal or senior partner. The guest curator/author is a mixed blessing, as anyone who works or has worked in a museum or gallery knows. Collaborative ventures need carefully devised rules if they are to be successful, and both parties need to respect the other's skills and be even-handed in achieving their joint goals. One obvious route would be secondments between museums and academic institutions, with both parties committed to mutually agreed work schedules that offer tangible results of benefit to both parties. The subject could be strengthened considerably if new and experimental partnerships can be arranged in which the different but complementary skills that academics and curators provide are accepted to be of joint importance. The history of dress and fashion is resilient and the next phase in how it is studied will undoubtedly be as challenging as any other in its long history.

Notes

Introduction

1 N Davies, *Europe, A History*, London 1997: pp. 427, 615, 774
2 C McDowell, *Costume 35*, London, 2001: p. 145
3 J Styles, 'Dress in History: reflections on a Contested Terrain', *Fashion Theory*: Vol. 2, Issue 4, p. 388
4 See L Taylor, *The Study of Dress History*, Manchester, 2002, which offers routes into the discipline but she does not address the problems inherent in museum provision and the threats to it not from academics but from under-funding.
5 C Breward, *The Culture of Fashion*, Manchester, 1995: p. 1

Chapter 1

1 F M Kelly and R Schwabe, *A Short History of Costume & Armour 1066–1800*, Newton Abbot, 1972: Vol. I, p. vi; Vol. II, p. v
2 A Tucker and T Kingswell, *Fashion, A Crash Course*, London, 2000: p. 13
3 *Ibid*: p. 11
4 *2002 New Books and Key Backlist*, Dress, Body, Culture Series, Oxford: Berg Publishers, 2002: p. 15
5 C Morris (ed.), *The Illustrated Journeys of Celia Fiennes 1685–c. 1712*, London, 1982: p. 119
6 *Ibid*: p. 214
7 *Ibid*: p. 196
8 A Ribeiro, 'Antiquarian Attitudes – Some Early Studies in the History of Dress', *Costume 28*, London, 1994: pp. 60–70
9 C Kohler and E von Sichart, *A History of Costume*, London, 1928: p. 5
10 *Ibid*: p. 5
11 J Stokes, *Resistible Theatres, Enterprise and experiment in the late nineteenth century*, London, 1972: p. 42 and p. 27. See also M F MacDonald, S G Galassi and A Ribeiro, *Whistler, Women & Fashion*, New Haven & London, 2003: p. 47
12 Stokes, op. cit: p. 42
13 T Hughes, *Dress Design, An Account of Costume for Artists and Dressmakers*, London, 1913: p. 34
14 *A Selected List of Batsford Books*, London, 1933: p. 16
15 Kelly and Schwabe, op. cit: Vol I, p. vi
16 *Ibid*: p. viii
17 *Ibid*: Vol II, pp. v–vi
18 *Ibid*: p. 83
19 J Laver, *The Literature of Fashion*, London, 1947: p. 4
20 *Ibid*: p. 52
21 M Davenport, *The Book of Costume*, New York, 1972: p. ix

22 Information from Susan North at the Victoria & Albert Museum, London, 2004
23 *Costume*, The Journal of the Costume Society, London, 1967: Vol. 1, No. 1, endpaper, unpaginated
24 *Ibid*: p. 1
25 *bid*: p. 2
26 C Ford, 'The National Film Archive, A Little Known Source of Costume History' in *Costume*, London, 1967: Vol. 1, No. 1, p. 5
27 *Ibid*: p. 5
28 The princess married the heir to the Swedish throne, later Gustav III (b. 1748, king 1771–92). He was a Francophile patron of the arts, especially fond of the theatre. His mother Queen Louisa Ulrika was a sister of Frederick the Great of Prussia, who presided over another Francophile court. Whoever prepared the princess's trousseau would have realized that ordering her dress from Paris or copying French styles would be wise. The marriage was not a success and ended with Gustav's assassination in 1792. This event provided Verdi with the plot for his 1859 opera *Un ballo in maschera*.

Chapter 2

1 R E M Wheeler, *London Museum Catalogue: No. 5 Costume*, London, 1946: p. 10
2 Wheeler, op. cit.: p. 9
3 For a feminist reassessment of Cunnington's theories see J Tozer, 'Cunnington's Interpretation of Dress', *Costume 20*, London, 1986: pp. 1–17
4 J Craik, *The Face of Fashion: Cultural Studies in Fashion*, London 1994: p. 46
5 J C Flügel, *The Psychology of Clothes*, London, 1930: p. 75
6 Laver, op. cit: p. 5
7 *Ibid*: p. 6
8 J Laver, *A Concise History of Costume*, London, 1968: p. 273
9 M Specter, 'Le Freak C'est Chic', *Observer Magazine*, 30 November 2003: p. 14
10 Cited in *Costume 18*, London, 1984: p. 125
11 'Aims and Scope', *Fashion Theory*, from 1997 onwards: unpaginated
12 Craik, op. cit: p. xii
13 *Ibid*: p. 6
14 *Ibid*: p. 7
15 Cited in J Munns and P Richards (eds), *The Clothes That Wear Us, Essays on Dressing and Transgressing in Eighteenth-Century Culture*, Newark and London, 1999: p. 11
16 Craik, op. cit: p. 10
17 E Wilson, Extract from an unattributed review on the back cover of the paperback edition of *The Culture of Fashion*, Manchester, 1995

18 A de la Haye and E Wilson, *Defining Dress, Dress as object, meaning and identity*, Manchester, 1999: p. 1
19 *Ibid*: pp. 7–8
20 'Aims and Scope', *Fashion Theory*, op. cit: unpaginated
21 A Warwick and D Cavallaro, *Fashioning the Frame, Boundaries, Dress and the Body*, Oxford, 1998: p. 109
22 B Burman and C Turbin, *Material Strategies, Dress and Gender in Historical Perspective*, Malden, MA, & Oxford, 2002: p. 1
23 *Ibid*: pp. 1–2
24 *Ibid*: p. 2
25 *Ibid*: p. 9

Chapter 3

1 *The Concise Oxford English Dictionary*, sixth edition, Oxford, 1976
2 *Eighteenth century to eBay: Family trail to accompany the Enlightenment Galleries*, British Museum, London, 2003: unpaginated.
3 A N Jones and P Stallybrass, *Renaissance Clothing and the Materials of Memory*, Cambridge, 2000. Jones and Stallybrass are Professors of Comparative Literature and examine a range of literary topics and inter-disciplinary studies, which they apply to dress and textiles. It is not a book on Renaissance Clothing per se.
4 P Byrde and P Brears, 'A Pair of James I's Gloves', *Costume 24*, London, 1990: pp. 34–42
5 T Wilkinson, *Memoirs of His Own Life*, cited in A M Nagler, *A Source Book in Theatrical History*, New York, 1959: p. 388. Wilkinson gives detailed if sometimes partisan descriptions of the costume system within the theatre in the second half of the 18th century.
6 J Arnold, *A Handbook of Costume*, London, 1973: contents, unpaginated.
7 *Victoria & Albert Museum*, London, 1991: p. 6
8 F Sheppard, *The Treasury of London's Past*, London, 1991: p. 20
9 *Victoria & Albert Museum*, op. cit: p. 53
10 The Victoria & Albert Museum website at *www.vam.ac.uk*
11 M and C H B Quennell, *A History of Everyday Things in England 1733–1851*, London, 1933: p.196; and C W Cunnington, *English Women's Clothing in the Nineteenth Century*, London, 1937: pp. 444–446
12 B M du Mortier, *Nothing but the best, Masterpieces from the Rijksmuseum's collection of costumes*, Amsterdam, 1996: unpaginated
13 *Ibid*.
14 *Ibid*.

15 Sheppard, op. cit: p. 27
16 *Ibid*: p. 83
17 *Ibid*: p. 88
18 *Ibid*: p. 104
19 *Ibid*: p. 112
20 Wheeler, op. cit: p. 10
21 P Weissman, 'The Costume Institute/The Early Years', *Vanity Fair*, The Metropolitan Museum of Art, 1977: unpaginated
22 *Ibid.*
23 *Ibid.*
24 A Depréaux, 'Paris Iñaugurates a Hall of Fame for the Mode', *Vogue*, Late May 1920: p. 56. I am indebted to Judith Watt for these *Vogue* references.
25 *Ibid*: p. 57
26 *Ibid.*
27 Tozer, op. cit: pp. 1–2
28 A Buck, 'The Gallery of English Costume, Platt Hall, Manchester', *Costume 6*, London, 1972: p. 72
29 Cunnington, op. cit: p. 444
30 *Ibid*: pp. 444–445
31 *Ibid*: p. 444
32 A Jarvis, 'An Agreeable Change from Ordinary Medical Diagnosis: The Costume Collection of Drs C. Willett and Phillis Cunnington', *Costume 33*, London, 1999: pp. 1–11. This is one of the two articles that did not find their way into the Methodology Special Issue of *Fashion Theory*, which resulted from the 1995 Manchester conference mentioned in the introduction to this book.
33 *Ibid*: p. 7
34 A Buck, *The Gallery of English Costume, Picture Book Number One, A Brief View*, Manchester, 1949: p. 3
35 Buck, *Costume 6*, op. cit: p. 73
36 M Beckett, 'Out of London's Fashion Museum', *Picture Post*, London, 21 April 1951: p. 18; I am indebted to Rosemary Harden for access to the archive papers at the Museum of Costume, Bath.
37 D Langley Moore, 'The Beginning of the Collection', *The So-Called Age of Elegance, Costume 1785–1820, Proceedings of the Fourth Annual Conference of the Costume Society*, London, 1971: p. 2
38 *Ibid.*
39 Photocopy of a fund-raising letter on behalf of the centre, dated 4 November 1952: Museum of Costume Archive, Bath
40 Proposal for a Museum of Costume, The Arts Council: Museum of Costume Archive, Bath; undated and unpaginated
41 Langley Moore, op. cit: p. 3
42 *Ibid*: p. 2

43 Olive Matthews Collection Archive, Chertsey Museum

Chapter 4
1 N Tarrant, 'The Real Thing: The Study of Original Garments in Britain since 1947', *Costume 33*, London, 1999: p. 21. This the second of the two articles that was not included in the Methodology Special Edition of *Fashion Theory* in 1998 but is based on a lecture given at the 1997 conference at Manchester.
2 This collection was based on one created by the collector Cecile Hummel and added to subsequently. Changed ideas about public presentation at Castle Howard led eventually to the sale of the collection in 2003. The Sotheby's sale catalogues for the October and November sales present a fascinating insight into the range and diversity of a collection, which contained garments from the 17th century up to the recent past.
3 S Blum, 'The Costume Institute/The Past Decade', *Vanity Fair*, The Metropolitan Museum of Art, New York, 1977: unpaginated
4 R A R, 'Obituary, Diana Vreeland', *Costume 24*, London, 1990: p. 152. This is a discreet analysis of her cavalier approach to collections, which I observed during a brief meeting at the Museum of London in the late 1970s. She had little respect for curators or what they curated.
5 N Tarrant, *The Development of Costume*, London, 1994: p. 2
6 Tarrant, *Costume 33* op. cit: pp. 14–15
7 *Ibid*: p. 21
8 I am indebted to Helen Wilkinson at The Museums Association for information on this project.
9 This information was received from Anthea Jarvis and Howard Smith of Manchester City Galleries, to whom I am indebted.
10 I am indebted for this information to Philip Warren at Leicestershire Museums, Arts and Records Service.
11 This information was received from Rosemary Harden at the Museum of Costume, Bath, and I am indebted to her for her help.
12 B Burman, Synopsis of the AHRB Research Project, Pockets of History, June 2003. I am indebted to Barbara Burman for information on this project.
13 *Ibid*
14 Correspondence with Rosemary Harden.

Chapter 5
1 Tozer, op. cit: p. 16
2 A Courrèges, 'Is Fashion an Art?', *The Metropolitan Museum of Art Bulletin*, New York, November 1967: p. 138
3 E N Lawrence and A S Cavallo, 'Sleuthing at the Seams', *The Metropolitan Museum of Art Bulletin*, New York, August/September 1971: pp. 22–31
4 J Ashelford, *The Art of Dress, Clothes and Society 1500–1914*, London, 1996: p. 98; and C MacLeod, *Painted Ladies, Women at the Court of Charles II*, London, 2001: pp. 57–58
5 S Stevenson and D Thomson, *John Michael Wright, The King's Painter*, Edinburgh, 1982: p. 30
6 G Ashton and I Mackintosh, *Royal Opera House Retrospective 1732–1982*, London, 1982: pp. 116–118 provides a useful discussion of the several versions of this painting in regard to theatre practice at the time.
7 Cited in Ashelford, op. cit: p.124
8 Cited in A Wilton, *The Swagger Portrait, Grand Manner Portraiture in Britain from Van Dyck to Augustus John 1630–1930*, London, 1992, p. 49
9 Cited in E Waterhouse, *Gainsborough*, London, 1966: p. 22
10 Cited in A Ribeiro, *Dress in Eighteenth Century Europe 1715–1789*, London, 1984: p163. This book contains a useful discussion on the pan-European fascination with masquerade costume in the 18th century.
11 Cited in Ashelford, op. cit: p. 136. She mentions that his housekeeper used the blue velvet of this suit to make cushions, indicating a complete lack of nostalgia for the suit.
12 Cited in Wilton, op. cit: p. 51
13 R Treble, *Great Victorian Pictures*, London, 1978: p.77
14 *Ibid*: p. 24
15 Wilton, op. cit: pp. 210–211
16 A Griffiths, *The Print in Stuart Britain 1603–1689*, London, 1998: p. 260
17 I am indebted to Harry Matthews for information about fashion illustration and collecting.
18 R Hyde and V Cumming, 'The Prints of Benjamin Read, Tailor and Printmaker', *Print Quarterly* XVII, 2000: pp. 262–284
19 Cited in S M Newton, *Health, Art & Reason, Dress Reformers of the 19ᵗʰ Century*, London, 1974: pp. 93–94
20 Hughes, op. cit: p. xiv
21 Cited in J Mulvagh, *Vogue History of 20ᵗʰ Century Fashion*, London, 1988: p. 86
22 Depréaux, op. cit: p. 56
23 P Weissman, *Fashion, Art, and Beauty*, op. cit: p. 151
24 T Hoving, *The Metropolitan Museum of Art Bulletin*, New York, August/September 1971: p. 1

25 C R Dodwell (ed.), *The Whitworth Art Gallery, The First Hundred Years*, Manchester, 1988: p. 5
26 *Ibid.*
27 P Wollen (ed.), *Addressing the Century, 100 Years of Art & Fashion*, London, 1998: unpaginated.
28 *Ibid*: p. 111
29 *Ibid.*
30 Lot 116 in the Sotheby's Passion for Fashion sale in London, 27 November 2003. An embroidered and lace inset black satin evening coat, c. 1912. The catalogue entry stated: 'This coat has traditionally believed to have been made by Paul Poiret'. It was bought by the Olive Matthews Collection at Chertsey Museum.
31 S Mower, 'Back to the fuchsia', interview with Zandra Rhodes, *Evening Standard*, London, 9 May 2003: p. 27
32 *Ibid.*

Chapter 6

1 John Nevinson, quoted in A Mansfield, *Ceremonial Costume*, London, 1980: p. 60
2 Cunnington, *Nineteenth Century*, op. cit: p. 169
3 Cunnington *Twentieth Century*, op. cit: p. 23
4 V Cumming, 'Pantomime and Pageantry, The Coronation of George IV', *London World City*, London, 1992: pp. 39–50; discusses tailoring and ceremonial dress relevant to this chapter.
5 S Stevenson and H Bennett, *Van Dyck in Checktrousers, Fancy Dress in Art and Life 1700-1900*, Edinburgh, 1978: p. 15; and S Rosenfeld, *The Theatre of the London Fairs in the 18ᵗʰ century*, Cambridge, 1960: p. 100
6 Cumming, 'Pantomime and Pageantry', op. cit: pp. 41–42
7 A Lansdell, 'A Guide to the Study of Occupational Costume in the Museums of England and Wales', in *Proceedings of the Seventh Annual Conference of the Costume Society 1973*, London, 1974: pp. 41–55
8 Cunnington and Beard, op. cit: p. 199
9 Cited in Mansfield, op. cit., p. 59.
10 *Ibid*: p. 60
11 *Ibid*: p. 61
12 K Balfour, 'Granny Knows Best', *The Telegraph Magazine*, London, 6 December 2003: p. 33
13 K Kay 'Heirlooms and graces', *You* Magazine (as part of *The Mail on Sunday*), London, 17 August 2003: p. 40
14 Advertisement, 'Bandoliers for musketeers, incorporating Stockings for Soldiers', *Living History Digest*, Poole, 2003: Vol. 21, No. 1, inside back cover
15 P Poppy, 'Fancy Dress? Costume for Re-enactment', *Costume 31*, London, 1997: p. 103

16 V Cumming, 'Costume or Clothes? Dressing the 1815 Season at the Sans Pareil Theatre', *Nineteenth Century Theatre and Film 29/2*, Manchester, 2003

Chapter 7

1 S Blum (ed.), *Victorian Fashions & Costumes from Harper's Bazaar: 1867–1898*, New York, 1974: p.3
2 V Cumming, 'Costume', *The Oxford Encyclopedia of Theatre and Performance, Vol. 1*, Oxford, 2003: p. 318
3 Cited in Nagler, op. cit: p. 239
4 *Ibid*: p. 240
5 *Ibid*: p. 392
6 *Ibid.*
7 *Ibid*: pp. 358, 398; see also J Gross, *Shylock, Four Hundred Years in the Life of a Legend*, London,1994: pp. 94–99
8 Nagler, *Ibid*: p. 414
9 *Ibid*: p. 397
10 *Ibid.*
11 *The Diary of Samuel Pepys*, edited by R Latham and W Matthews, London, 1995: Vol. VIII, p. 91
12 *Ibid*: p. 101
13 Nagler, op. cit: pp. 229–230
14 J Shattock (ed.), *The Oxford Guide to British Women Writers*, Oxford, 1994: pp. 97–98
15 Rosenfeld, op. cit: p. 115
16 G Rowell, *The Victorian Theatre 1792–1914*, 2nd. Edition, Cambridge, 1978: p. 70
17 E Ransome (ed.), *The Terrific Kemble*, London, 1978: p.124
18 *Ibid*: p. 176
19 Viola and Rosalind are not true breeches roles; the term is not applied to parts within which actresses adopt male disguise while performing a female role.
20 V Cumming, 'Ellen Terry: An Aesthetic Actress and her Costumes', *Costume 21*, London, 1987: pp. 67–74
21 F Wills, *W. G. Wills*, London, 1898: p. 161
22 Cumming, 'Ellen Terry', op. cit: illustrates one of the Doucet dresses.
23 M R Holmes, *Stage Costume and Accessories in the London Museum*, London, 1968: p. 7. This is a useful if now dated catalogue to one of the important collections of stage costume in the United Kingdom.
24 'Our Ladies Pages', *The Sketch*, London, 23 January 1895: p. 646
25 T Pepper, *High Society Photographs 1897–1914*, London, 1998: p. 58 shows Lillie Langtry stretched out on a chaise longue in one of these Worth dresses.
26 Nagler, op. cit: p. 413
27 Ransome, op. cit: p. 87

28 *Ibid.*
29 Rosenfeld, op. cit: p. 15
30 Rowell, op. cit: p. 28
31 R Jackson (ed.), *Victorian Theatre*, London, 1989: p. 311
32 *Ibid.*
33 K M Rogers, *18th- and 19th- Century British Drama*, New York, 1996: p. 9
34 H Pearson, *The Last Actor Managers*, London, 1974: pp. 29–30
35 Rosenfeld, op. cit: p. 54
36 *Ibid*: p. 60
37 *Ibid*: p. 99
38 J Coleman (ed.), *Memoirs of Samuel Phelps*, London, 1898: p. 48
39 *Ibid*: p. 167; see also Holmes, op. cit: p. 29
40 *The Autobiography of Sir John Martin-Harvey*, London,1933: p. 45
41 Jackson, op. cit: p. 120
42 M and S Bancroft, *The Bancrofts: Recollections of Sixty Years*, London, 1909: p. 9
43 Jackson, op. cit: p. 127
44 Martin-Harvey, op. cit: p. 122
45 *Ibid.*

Conclusion

1 Professor Harold Bloom quoted in J Walsh, 'The Saturday Profile, Harold Bloom – a vortex of passions', *The Independent*, London, 28 February 2004: p. 44

Appendix:
concepts, disciplines and people

This short appendix offers a starting point from which to explore some of the new ideas in the study of dress history and the clothed and unclothed body. The entries are as short as possible in order to indicate how or why the concepts, disciplines and people might have relevance to dress historians. Each word in **bold type** in an individual entry relates to another entry. A good introduction to the early theorists, and with an excellent bibliography of more recent work of a theoretical nature, can be found in Michael Carter's *Fashion Classics, from Carlyle to Barthes*, published in 2003.

Adorno, Theodor (1903–69)

German philosopher, sociologist and musicologist and highly influential member of the **Frankfurt School**. His work with his colleague Max Horkheimer, *Dialectic of the Enlightenment* (1947, English translation 1972) considered the malaise of modernity and proposed the idea that even in democratic societies mass culture could reduce the population to unquestioning social conformity. His work considered concepts of reality and the role of art and music within repressive social structures.

Anthropology

Term taken from the Greek, meaning the study of humankind. This became an accepted academic discipline in the 19th century but it widened its remit in the 1960s to investigate how people conduct their lives in all types of social and cultural contexts throughout the world.

The French anthropologist and ethnographer Claude Lévi-Strauss offered a new approach to the discipline by applying **structuralist** models derived from **linguistics**. His theories investigated a range of social and cultural elements such as myths, symbols and totemism. His ideas were influential but his work tended to underplay historical processes and to ignore the constructive role of the individual in society.

In the 1970s interpretive anthropology emerged from the American tradition of Cultural Anthropology. This approach considered how individuals assigned symbolic meanings within cultures, but the process attracted criticism as it suggested that anthropologists might impose their own meanings across cultural groups. Subsequently ethnographic writing offered a more reflexive approach devising a process of dialogue between anthropologist and informant. The impact of **postmodernism** has led to some anthropologists being overly reflexive in their approach. The widespread influence of this self-critical attitude towards gathering evidence and interpreting it, and the expansion of anthropological enquiry into other disciplines, including **cultural history**, **gender studies** and literary theory, has had a powerful impact that is also felt within the study of dress and textiles.

Antiquarianism

A cultural movement, which, from the 16th century onwards, emphasized the need to collect, preserve and study historical artefacts and documents. The idea that paintings, museums and novels could represent the past with some degree of accuracy, through emphasizing display and interpretation of this evidence allowed the theatre and performance to become natural allies in this process. The scenery and costumes of a thoroughly researched historical play allowed the transformation of such evidence into a live re-enactment as opposed to merely a literary or pictorial representation. Even in its heyday antiquarianism attracted criticism and is now a pejorative term within academic circles.

Barthes, Roland (1925–80)

Associated with **structuralism**, **semiotics**, **poststructuralism** and **postmodernism**, Barthes' work questioned how meaning was produced in works of art. The English translation of a group of his essays *Image – Music – Text* (1977) brought his short essay 'The Death of the Author' to the attention of English-speaking literary theorists. 'The Death of the Author' can be perceived to be of interest to dress historians because clothing has no distinct author – even if designed and styled to suit one individual, a process undertaken by major fashion designers, it cannot avoid taking on the qualities of others who then wear all or part of the garments. His interest in fashion predated his book *The Fashion System* and is discussed in Michael Carter's book *Fashion Classics*.

Baudrillard, Jean (1929–)

French theorist and one of the most influential figures in discussions about **postmodernism**. His first book *The System of Objects* was published in 1968. There were many influences upon his early thinking. These include: Marx's critique of modernity; Walter **Benjamin's** ideas that mass reproduction reduced the significance of authenticity and originality; Henri Lefebvre's search for signs of Marxist revolution in all aspects of life; Guy Debord's view that spectacle and commodity dominate social life; Marshall McLuhan's interpretation of the impact of media on society and consciousness.

Central to his work is the view that everyone has become so saturated with visual imagery and media effects that the world can only be experienced through this media-devised filter of ideas, places and things. His work is cross-disciplinary, encompassing **linguistics**, philosophy, sociology, political theory and science fiction, within which his analysis of film and television is one element. He uses the term simulation to describe a world in which no originality or reality remains, only simulation. Simulations are emancipated from reference to reality but are part of everyone's lives. His work has been informed by theories about language and meaning as much as theories of media and society, which link him closely to **structuralism** and **poststructuralism**.

Benjamin, Walter (1892–1940)

German philosopher, literary critic and social theorist and a member of the **Frankfurt School**. His essay 'The Work of Art in the Age of Mechanical Reproduction' (1936) was widely influential. He believed that the use of new technologies could remove art from elite circles of moneyed patronage and make them widely available. This work irritated Theodor **Adorno** who preferred the view that autonomous art forms are more powerful than those found in the mass media.

Body

All societies see the human body as more than a merely physical organism. It is perceived as the focus of ideas about its psychological and social significance. **Anthropologists**, for example, view the body as a statement of an individual's place in society. The manner in which it is adorned, clothed and marked can express ethnic, **gender**, status and religious identity.

The body can also be seen as a microcosm of society, with the rules and taboos surrounding parts of the body mirroring social or cosmological principles. It can also be viewed as a metaphor for society; the **structuralist** Mary Douglas believes that the body can be seen as representing the body politic.

The complexity of interpretations range from the purely philosophical to concrete areas, both of which interest writers on dress and appearance. The latter subject matter might include body building, body decoration, body image, body language, body mutilation, body shape, body weight and so forth.

Cixous, Hélène (1937–)

French theorist, literary scholar, novelist and playwright. She rose to prominence in the 1970s as one of four French feminists (see also **Irigaray** and **Kristeva**) who developed the linguistic process known as *écriture feminine*. Cixous used this as a way of subverting masculine language and resisting strategies that define woman as the Other. This is the motif in her influential essay 'Laugh of the Medusa'. Her first successful play *Portrait of Dora* (1976) is a feminist interpretation of Freud's famous case study.

Cultural history

The separation of cultural history from anthropological or social science fields is a comparatively recent development in academic circles. Cultural history considers both visual and written evidence from all available sources of information and treats it analytically and contextually. It opposes the traditional view of culture as a progressive European movement of intellectual achievement that produced accepted forms of 'high culture' in the fine and applied arts, literature, the theatre etc. The traditional view was challenged by investigations into counter-culture, subculture and mass culture. The last was a formal acknowledgment of the contributions of the majority of the population rather than the minority of elite patrons and providers of culture. The history of dress is often taught within departments of cultural history with a particular emphasis on **gender**, cultural diversity and social inclusivity.

Deconstruction

This is a technique principally associated with the French philosopher Jacques **Derrida**. It allows for intellectual scepticism about all and every type of received idea, but is particularly influential within the field of literary criticism. The starting point is that a literary text has many meanings and that the term 'meaning' is a diffuse and fragmentary one. The process of deconstruction does not seek a unified and coherent intention within a text but concentrates on individual elements and on any gaps, dislocations and disjunctions found within it.

In the 1990s the term deconstructionists was used for a group of fashion designers, including Ann Demeulemeester, Helmut Lang and Martin Margiela, who broke down the traditional parts of dress and reformed them, often using clothing as artistic and/or social statements.

Derrida, Jacques (1930–)

The most influential of modern French philosophers. He came to prominence in the late 1960s, but in the English-speaking world his major contribution has been in the field of literary criticism. The principal distinction between modern French philosophy and Anglo-American philosophy is that the former believe that philosophy should be more akin to art and literature whereas the latter revolves around the rigour and precision of the natural sciences.

His early works, written between 1967 and 1972, provide an extensive series of commentaries on texts by key thinkers within the Western tradition. In these commentaries he developed a **poststructuralist** blend of philosophy, **linguistics** and literary analysis to texts called **deconstruction**. His work emphasizes aspects of language often neglected by philosophers, for example, ambiguity, indeterminacy, pun and metaphor. Derrida is frequently cited by exponents of the new dress history, who have a background training in literature and sociology and who combine these interests with **feminist** and **gender** studies.

Discourse

A term used in the fields of art history, critical theory, **linguistics**, literary theory and sociology. The application of the term has somewhat different uses depending upon the discipline. The **Frankfurt School** of critical sociology developed the form of analysis called critical theory in order to understand and explain social reality by evaluating and criticizing society's understanding of itself.

In linguistics and literary theory the term discourse is associated with **Michel Foucault** and his circles. Foucault advocated the use of 'intellectual archaeology' to study social attitudes and structures by **deconstructing** the discourses involved. Within literary theory the study of discourse is a method by which creative work is examined in terms of the intellectual ideas of past societies and the groups or individuals within them, thereby shedding light on the content and meaning of works created within those societies.

Feminism

A political **discourse** that examines relationships between women and men; promoting women's struggle for self-determination against ideas of patriarchy and sexism. It encompasses theories that promote sexual, social and political equality for women, although the emphasis depends upon the particular theories and methods of analysis used within specific feminist ideologies. Its definitions relate to class, nationality, race and sexuality as much as they do to ideology or philosophy.

Its early history can be traced back to the late 18th century but the significant mid-20th-century figure is the French philosopher and writer Simone de Beauvoir. Her publication *The Second Sex* (1949) defines the problem, 'One is not born, but rather becomes a woman'; indicating that woman is 'Other' and therefore negative to the male's positive status. This view became a major concern of late-20th-century feminists like **Cixous** and **Irigaray** and influenced the development of their work.

Since the early 1970s feminism has developed a variety of critical discourses that affect all aspects of life, and its influence has spread beyond political and social inequalities into personal relationships and sexual identity. Feminist criticism is found in most academic disciplines and theories of feminism, sex and **gender** have explored the historical roots of women's oppression, the development of gender roles in social, psychological and emotional development, and gender stereotyping in forms of cultural representation. The different approaches to both defining and countering sex-role stereotyping have resulted in many feminist theories and practices. What they have in common is an emphasis on the fact that women have been classified and described in a manner that limits their spheres of influence within patriarchal societies.

The writing of history was examined for the patriarchal attitudes hidden within it, and new historical perspectives revised conventional histories, revealing possibilities for change in women's position in society. Histories of and for women were developed and this had an impact upon conventional approaches to historical research.

Psychoanalysis has been a significant element in feminist theories since the 1970s. While rejecting Freud's views of the inadequacies of women, some French, British and American feminists accept Freud's model of the development of the child, which defines sexual difference as culturally acquired, and have developed this idea to suit feminist agendas of change. Feminist readings of traditional dress history tend to emphasize the outdated views of male dress historians such as James Laver and C W Cunnington.

Foucault, Michel (1926–84)

French philosopher principally associated with **discourse** analysis. He used this method for examining how systems function in culture, ideology, language and society, and the way in which that functioning reflects and sustains power and those who exercise power. He rejected the idea that power can be owned or used in the interests of a group or an individual. He argued that power is an invisible force, exercised rather than possessed, and his work examined the intricate links between power and knowledge. He shared certain ideas with **poststructuralists** such as **Barthes** and **Derrida**, but differed from them in two significant ways. He retained the idea of the author and used historical periods within which he undertook 'intellectual archaeology'. His methods studied the structure of a society or its attitudes towards such factors as madness, punishment and sexuality by **deconstructing** the **discourse** involved.

Frankfurt School

A group of German social theorists originally associated with the Institute for Social Research at Frankfurt University, which was founded in 1923. The Institute closed in 1934 and several members settled in America until the early 1950s. The group included **Theodor Adorno**, **Walter Benjamin**, Max Horkheimer and Herbert Marcuse.

They attempted to re-define Marxist theory in the light of more recent developments in capitalist and communist states, trying to reposition Marx's ideas within the complexities of modern culture. Their work, separately and together, is significant to students of the mass media and popular culture. They looked at the impact of mass consumer culture and how it could be dehumanized by technology manipulated in favour of the status quo rather than change.

Gender

The basic definition is concerned with anatomical or biological differences between female and male. **Anthropologists**, **feminists** and sociologists have developed new methods for considering gender in society. They look at cultural

variations in the construction of gender; these can include concepts of the **body**, ideas about sexuality, and the ways in which gender roles are conditioned by society. Studies within and across academic disciplines have identified the study of dress and fashion as of particular interest, particularly in regard to how clothing is an important element in the construction of identity.

Irigaray, Luce (1932–)

French feminist philosopher, linguist and psychoanalyst who studied with **Lacan** but was expelled from his Vincennes school as she disagreed with his views on women's sexuality. *Speculum and the Other Woman* (1974) is a critical reading of the history of Western philosophy as 'the master discourse', which discusses the exclusion or suppression of the feminine and the maternal and the bias towards masculinity. In *This Sex Which is Not One* (1977) she contends that women are absent from representation since they can only mimic men's language and cannot speak autonomously. Her texts construct a version of feminine subjectivity by using a strategic and symbolic positioning of Woman as Other.

Lacan, Jacques (1901–81)

French psychoanalyst whose unorthodox reading of the work of Sigmund Freud generated controversies and splits within the psychoanalytic movement. Lacan's claim, drawn from the linguistic ideas of **Saussure** and Jakobson, is that the unconscious is 'structured like a language'. He defined language as a culturally constructed order that positioned women linguistically and sexually as subservient to men. His work can be seen as reinforcing **gender** difference and male superiority, but his insistence upon the cultural construction of language also offered the opportunity for resisting cultural norms.

Kristeva, Julia (1941–)

French literary critic, philosopher and psychoanalyst. She was born in Bulgaria but has been based in Paris since the 1960s, where she has worked with **Derrida** and others in the intellectual group Tel Quel. She drew from Marxist theory, Russian formalism, **structuralism** and psychoanalysis to provide an interdisciplinary approach to questions of subjectivity.

Kristeva is concerned with the relationship between writing, culture and subjectivity. She uses the term **semiotic** to describe the character of communication available to the pre-Oedipal, pre-language child, which survives in repressed form in adults and which can, in turn, be used as a means of analyzing texts and images. Her theoretical exploration of literary texts, creativity and language acquisition has widened to include political, sexual, philosophical and **linguistic** issues. Some of her work has been in **feminist** philosophy; some in aesthetics, **cultural** studies and psychoanalysis.

Linguistics

The scientific study of language. **Saussure** initiated a revolution in linguistics when he emphasized the importance of a language system in its existing form rather than just considering processes of language change.

Material culture

This term, originally found in archaeology, has been applied to other types of artefacts held in public and private collections. It is a widely accepted method of presenting artefacts within a social context rather than in chronological type sequences that merely trace change but do not explain the causes and purposes of such changes. Within a number of museums, collections of dress and textiles are curated as part of the evidence of material culture rather than as evidence of applied or decorative arts traditions and skills. The two methods are complementary rather than antithetical.

Modernism and postmodernism

These terms are used across a range of the arts to identify and/or describe a variety of chronological and stylistic movements. The term modernism was used throughout the 20th century but at the close of the century the terms modernism/postmodernism indicated contrasting movements and ideas. In literature, modernist writers are considered to be those who experiment with language and forms or use non-realist approaches to their work, such as James Joyce, Virginia Woolf, Ezra Pound, W B Yeats and dramatists such as Pirandello, T S Eliot, Samuel Beckett and Jean Genet. Within the visual arts futurism, dada, constructivism and surrealism are modernist movements. Modernism developed as new ideas in one area imitated the strategies in another already defined as modernist.

Postmodernism is not the successor to modernism; it is a movement opposed to high-modernist culture. It emerged in the arts, design and literature in the late 1960s and blurs boundaries between genres and historical periods, adopting intercultural forms and offering an eclectic mix of styles and forms that provide entry points into debates about contemporary life. Its range is such that any introductory text on postmodernism will encompass most of the movements and names given in this appendix.

Saussure, Ferdinand de (1857–1913)

A Swiss national who studied languages at Leipzig in Germany and taught in Paris before returning to teach at Geneva University. His course in general **linguistics** was much admired by colleagues and students and after his death they collated their notes to publish his major work, the *Cours de linguistique générale* in 1916. His departure from previously accepted approaches to language and his belief in the importance of signs and their social and political dimensions are crucial to **structuralist** and **postmodernist** theories.

Semiotics

From the Greek, meaning study of signs. The founder of semiotics was the American linguistic philosopher C S Pierce (1839–1914). He identified three types of sign, the iconic (a sign that represents its meaning directly), the indexical (only identifiable by association) and the symbolic (a meaning established by convention, e.g. red for danger). Originally these categories were mainly applied to language, but the Swiss linguistic philosopher Ferdinand de **Saussure** broadened this approach to encompass all methods of communication in what he called semiology. Saussure's ideas became applicable well beyond **linguistics**. They are essential to literary criticism, especially psychoanalytic criticism and **structuralism**, and they are influential in **anthropology**, media studies and sociology. **Barthes** applied **structuralist** techniques to systems of signs or objects other than language, most notably in *The Fashion System*.

Simmel, Georg (1895–1918)

German social philosopher who wrote about fashion and on issues of modernity. He has influenced **postmodernist** writing with his work on the impact of cities on traditional attitudes towards space and social interaction. His work in this area is often discussed alongside that of the French writer Charles Baudelaire. His work on fashion and class and fashion and modernity are discussed in Michael Carter's *Fashion Classics*.

Structuralism and poststructuralism

Influential branches of 20th-century European and American theories and criticism in the arts. Structuralism, the modernist critical movement, developed in Prague in the 1930s among a group of Czech literary scholars and Russian émigrés, including Roman Jakobson. Their ideas about language and literary techniques drew upon work undertaken by Russian formalists in the 1920s.

The anthropologist Claude Lévi-Strass laid the foundations for the French structuralism of the 1940s and 1950s. He found a more rigorous and scientific model for anthropology in **linguistics** and expanded upon **Saussure's** ideas. Structuralism is closely linked to **semiotics**, the system of analyzing signs and their meanings. Lévi-Strauss tried to analyze the internal structures of social relationships and cultural practices, for example in language, art, myth, ritual, marriage and kinship rules, by isolating what he perceived to be systematic patterns of the binary opposites that constitute them and the inter-relationship of their component parts. These theories made their way to England and America in the 1960s and early 1970s as Lévi-Strauss's works became available in translation.

Within various academic disciplines there were objections to the dominance of structuralism. This led to the development of various other critical hypotheses: **deconstruction (Derrida)**, psychoanalytical theory (**Lacan**), Marxist analysis, and new work within **feminism**, new historicism and post-colonial studies. All these approaches are poststructural, but are not necessarily in agreement with each other. A number of scholars who originally accepted structuralism, for example **Barthes**, **Lacan** and **Foucault**, turned to approaches that allowed for uncertainties, incoherencies, and indeterminate and irresolvable issues. These found their way into **postmodernist** practice in the arts, in which poststructural theory and criticism are essential components.

Glossary

Aesthetic dress: a description of the ideas promoted by a small group of artistically inclined and influential women who wore an alternative style of clothing to the highly structured women's dress of the 1870s onwards. The style is characterized by naturally dyed, soft flowing dresses with a vaguely medieval appearance. Although it provoked ridicule, cartoons and a Gilbert and Sullivan opera, this idea presages the simpler fashions of the early 20th century.

Bag-wig: the small silk bag within which the queue of a powdered wig was enclosed at the back of the neck. A flat silk bow covered the tie strings.

Baize: woollen fabric similar to thin serge (q.v.).

Bloomers: a term usually applied to the loose, Turkish-style trousers adopted by Mrs Amelia Bloomer in the early 1850s. In fact the complete outfit consisted of a fitted bodice, full, knee-length skirt and Turkish trousers. The fitted bodice and skirt resembled those worn by professional dancers. It caused criticism and provoked many cartoons, although few women actually wore these garments. The baggy knee-length cycling breeches that women wore in the 1890s were also called Bloomers.

Bone lace: lace made on a pillow with bone bobbins; often also called bobbin lace.

Callimanco: woollen fabric which could be plain, striped or checked but had a glazed finish.

Codpiece: the padded and prominent pouch at the centre-front juncture of male trunk hose in the 16th century.

Cravat: long neckcloth of lawn, muslin or silk folded around the neck and tied at the front in a bow or knot.

Crinoline: stiffened petticoat, the stiffening of crin (horsehair) and wool, but after 1856 a lightweight structure of whalebone or metal hoops worn under the petticoat and dress.

Directoire: description of the high-waisted styles of female dress between the late 1880s and 1890s that paid homage to the look of female clothes between 1795–99.

Duffel coat: short coat of heavy woollen fabric fastened by wooden toggles and loops, with or without a hood. Worn by British naval personnel in World War II; surplus stock was sold after the war and became a staple overcoat for both sexes.

Hoop: term used for an 18th-century under-petticoat with elongated sides formed by ribs of cane, wire or whalebone.

Hussar: term taken from military regiments and applied to the characteristic frogging and braiding on a jacket.

Nightgown: a loose gown worn informally by both sexes before they change into formal wear.

Serge: either a loosely woven twilled worsted or a loosely woven twilled flannel with worsted warp and wool weft.

Steinkerk: a long cravat (q.v.) edged with lace, loosely knotted at the neck with the ends threaded through a buttonhole or pinned to the side. A casual style associated with the battle of the same name in 1692.

Stomacher: the V-shaped, usually decorative panel that was pinned between the fronts of a woman's open bodice.

Tammy: a fine worsted fabric with a glazed finish.

Vandyke dress: a style of masquerade costume for men and women that appropriated some of the features of dress seen in Van Dyck's portraits of the 1630s. In the theatre Vandyke dress was a variant of this style but simplified for the purposes of exaggerated gesture and movement.

Windsor uniform: a style of uniform in navy, red and gold introduced by George III for his closest circle of family and courtiers. By the 19th century it was worn only by men and came in two versions: full-dress or informal. The coat and knee breeches of the informal version are occasionally worn by members of the royal family for state functions at Windsor Castle.

Zouave: style of coat or jacket for men and women based on the design worn by Algerian Zouave soldiers in the Italian war of 1859.

Select bibliography

The arrangement of bibliographies varies from author to author. Some divide their entries by original documents, primary and secondary sources; others sub-divide further placing articles and catalogues in additional categories. This is a select bibliography only; many works referred to in the text or the footnotes are not included and the listing does not differentiate by categories. A publication date in brackets indicates when the book first appeared.

Arch, N, and Marschner, J, *Splendour at Court, Dressing for Royal Occasions since 1700*, London, 1987

Arnold, J, Patterns of Fashion, *Englishwomen's dresses and their construction c. 1660–1860*, London, 1972 (1964)

Arthur, L, *Embroidery 1600–1700 at the Burrell Collection*, Glasgow, 1995

Barnes, R M, *Military Uniforms of Britain and the Empire*, London, 1972 (1960)

Blakemore, C, and Jennett, S (eds), *The Oxford Companion to The Body*, Oxford, 2001

Blum, S (ed.), *Ackermann's Costume Plates, Women's Fashions in England, 1818–1828*, New York, 1978

Blum, S (ed.), *Victorian Fashions & Costumes from Harper's Bazar: 1867–1898*, New York, 1974

Bradfield, N, *Costume in Detail, Women's Dress 1730–1930*, London, 1981 (1968)

Buck, A, *Dress in Eighteenth-Century England*, London, 1979

Buck, A, *Victorian Costume*, Bedford, 1984

Cobley, P, and Jansz, L, *Semiotics for Beginners*, Cambridge, 1997

Coleridge, N, *The Fashion Conspiracy*, London, 1989 (1988)

Crawford, P, and Gowing, L (eds), *Women's Worlds in Seventeenth-Century England*, London, 2000

Crowther, A, *Madame Clapham, The Celebrated Dressmaker*, Kingston upon Hull Museums & Art Galleries, no date

Cumming, V, *Royal Dress*, London, 1989

Cunnington, C W & P E, and Beard, C, *A Dictionary of English Costume 900–1900*, London, 1960

Foster, V, *Bags and Purses*, London, 1992 (1982)

Ginsburg, M, *An Introduction to Fashion Illustration*, London: Victoria & Albert Museum, 1980

de la Haye, A, *Fashion Source Book, A Visual Reference to Twentieth Century Fashion*, London, 1988

Holland, V, *Hand Coloured Fashion Plates 1770 to 1899*, London, 1988 (1955)

Honderich, T (ed.), *The Oxford Companion to Philosophy*, Oxford, 1995

Ironside, J, *A Fashion Alphabet*, London, 1968

Keenan, B, *The Women We Wanted to Look Like*, New York, 1978

Levitt, S, *Victorians Unbuttoned, Registered Designs for Clothing, their Makers and Wearers, 1839–1900*, London, 1986

Ed. Lynam, R, *Paris Fashion, The Great Designers and their Creations*, London, 1972

McDowell, C, *McDowell's Directory of Twentieth Century Fashion*, London, 1984

McLeish, K (ed.), *Bloomsbury Guide to Human Thought*, London, 1993

Mansfield, A, *Ceremonial Costume*, London, 1980

O' Connor, D and Granger-Taylor, H, *Colour & the Calico Printer*, Farnham, 1982

O'Hara Callan, G, *Dictionary of Fashion and Fashion Designers*, London, revised edition 1998

Pritchard, F, *Fortuny fabrics*, Manchester, 1998

Ribeiro, A, *Dress in Eighteenth Century Europe 1715–1789*, London, 1984

Ribeiro, A, *Dress and Morality*, London, 1986

Ribeiro, A, and Cumming, V, *The Visual History of Costume*, London, 1989

Rowley, C, *Costume in Chertsey Museum 1700–1800*, Chertsey, 1976

Rushton, P, *18th Century Costume in the National Museums and Galleries on Merseyside*, Liverpool, 1999

Schoeser, M, *Printed Handkerchiefs*, London, 1988

Steele, V, *Paris Fashion, A Cultural History*, Oxford, 1998 (1988)

Tarrant, N, *Smocks in the Buckinghamshire County Museum*, Aylesbury, 1976

Thomas, R (ed.), *Frocks and Fripperies, Ladies' Dress and Accessories From the 17th – 20th Century*, Lincoln, 1995

Thornton, P, *Baroque and Rococo Silks*, London, 1965

Ward, G, *Postmodernism*, London, 1997

Wilson, S (ed.), *Simply Stunning, The Pre-Raphaelite Art of Dressing*, Cheltenham, 1996

Index